ANSWERING THE CALL

STEVEN SHEPARD

| ANSWERING THE CALL |

How Brian Canfield Shaped Canada's Telecom Industry

Figure.1

Vancouver / Berkeley

Published simultaneously as *Répondre à l'appel :
l'influence de Brian Canfield sur les télécommunications
au Canada*

Cataloguing data available from Library and
Archives Canada
ISBN 978-1-927958-31-5 (hbk.)
ISBN 978-1-927958-33-9 (ebook)
ISBN 978-1-927958-32-2 (pdf)

Editing by Barbara Pulling
Copy editing by Judy Phillips
Index by François Trahan

Design by Jessica Sullivan

Jacket photograph: Brian Canfield, a reassuring
presence during the years he spent at TELUS.

Printed and bound in Canada by Friesens
Distributed in the U.S. by Publishers Group West

Figure 1 Publishing Inc.
Vancouver BC Canada
www.figure1pub.com

Contents

Introduction xv

1
BEGINNINGS 1

2
RANK AND FILE 21

3
THE FORMATIVE
YEARS 35

4
INTO THE
C-SUITE 53

5
A FOCUS ON
PEOPLE 71

6
PIVOTAL
MOMENTS 85

7
BUILDING A MODEL
OF TRANSPARENT
GOVERNANCE 99

8
GIVING BACK 117

9
THE FUTURE
IS FRIENDLY 127

References 139
Acknowledgements 141
Photo Permissions 143
Index 145

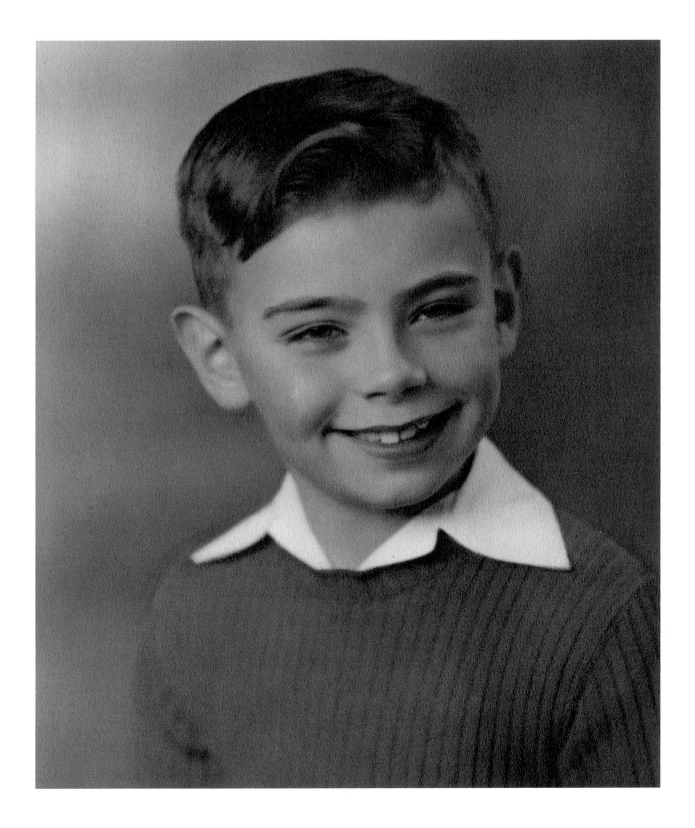

Introduction

IT'S A COMMONLY held position among those who study leadership that great executives—those held in high esteem as powerful motivators, organizational geniuses, and visionaries—benefited from certain advantages during their early lives. The list of these advantages is diverse: the enterprise superstars came from families who had multigenerational history in the company; they graduated from the best schools with degrees in management, finance, economics, strategy, or some combination of the same; they had influential parents who modelled executive behaviour and taught them how to play the game.

At the very least, they were blessed with driven, Type A personalities.

The fact is, though, these generalizations don't always apply. Some of the most revered leaders in the world came from humble beginnings. Many children who should have grown up to be industry titans, based on their education, family history, and economic situation, didn't do so. Good genetics, executive coaching, superior education, and benevolent nepotism certainly help, but they are not requirements for executive success. A careful examination of successful leaders does yield one similarity, though, a characteristic that Thomas

Edison captured in this defining quote: "The three great essentials to achieve anything worthwhile are, first, hard work; second, stick-to-itiveness; third, common sense."

Which brings us to Brian Canfield.

Brian Canfield joined BC Tel in 1956 as an apprentice equipment installer. He had no intention of becoming the chief executive of the company; all he wanted was a fair paycheque for an honest day's work. Fifty-eight years later, he retired from TELUS as chairman of the corporation. He didn't earn his high school diploma until many years after joining BC Tel, and never formally graduated from university, yet he was a gifted, visionary, and widely respected executive leader who oversaw the creation of the first national multimodal telephone company in Canada.

For all his successes, Brian didn't set out initially to climb the corporate ladder. He didn't come from a telephone company family, as so many employees did in the 1950s and early 1960s. He had no formal exposure to telecommunications; wasn't trained in the field through the military, as many were; and didn't have a degree in engineering or electronics. Yet he absorbed technical knowledge and skills breathtakingly fast. What he didn't learn on the job he sought out and taught himself, no matter how complex, difficult, or arcane the subject.

Brian was an only child whose father worked in a mill and whose mother was a music teacher. Like his parents, he worked hard, gave his all as a dedicated employee, and earned every penny he was paid.

Brian definitely wasn't the typical 1950s "organization man" that comedian Bob Newhart poked fun at; however, he was the employee who did what was asked of him no matter how demeaning the job. Some positions that others might have coveted Brian left after a few weeks because the work didn't engage him—and therefore he couldn't be as effective an employee as he was committed to being. By his own admission, he could be impatient and sometimes impetuous on the job. He would freely question the most respected authority, but always with facts in hand to back up his challenge.

In many ways, the story of BC Tel, including the merger and governance that helped create the modern-day TELUS, is the story of Brian Canfield. The two are inextricably intertwined, and for good reason: together, the man and the company redefined an entire industry and gave Canada the definition of good corporate citizenship, community leadership, transparency in organizational governance, and technological excellence.

Brian Canfield joined BC Tel right out of high school and rose through the ranks to the highest levels of executive leadership, serving as TELUS CEO and then as chairman of the corporation. Over the years, he became as legendary for his modesty as for his industry acumen. At all times, he was driven to do the right thing for TELUS, for the employees who worked for him, for the shareholders, and for Canada. He lived by a vision of a

TELUS
the future is friendly®

Thank you, Brian.

Thank you for your remarkable contributions to Canada's telecommunications industry throughout your legendary 58-year career with our company.

You have helped to revolutionize the way our society communicates, conducts business and accesses information.

You have also always exemplified our commitment to give where we live.

We wish you the very best as you retire and we are pleased to honour you with the Chairman Emeritus distinction.

The TELUS team

higher calling: to build a national service provider focused first and foremost on the customer, resulting in the creation of healthy nationwide competition, better pricing, and more innovative products and services. He bid the company a final farewell on May 8, 2014, but his legacy lives on.

Open letter to Brian Canfield on the date of his retirement, thanking him for his many contributions after a remarkable fifty-eight-year career.

CHAPTER 1

BEGINNINGS

THE CITY OF New Westminster (or New West, as it is known to its citizens) squats on the southeastern flank of the Burrard Peninsula, anchoring the peninsula to the west-flowing Fraser River. Long before European settlers arrived in the area, the Kwantlen First Nation people lived in two communities in the area, Skaiametl and Qayqayt. Skaiametl stood on the Surrey side of the Fraser River; Qayqayt, in the area that would ultimately become New Westminster.

The New Westminster town site was chosen initially for its strategic location. In the early nineteenth century, gold was discovered in the Fraser Canyon. So rich were the gold fields and so widespread the mania about them that local residents worried American miners would attempt to take over the golden spoils. The magnitude of concern about invasion from the south was so great that in 1858 regional governor James Douglas requested aid from the British government. In response, the Royal Engineers, led by Colonel Richard Clement Moody, were dispatched from England to repel the potential raiders. A hundred and fifty-four years later, TELUS would have similar concerns about a potential raider, this time an opportunistic investor.

FACING:
Columbia Street in winter, 1948. This was during the time that it was known as the "Golden Mile." Numerous businesses can be seen, including Copp The Shoe Man, Royal City Cafe, and Sanguine's Jewelers.

The company wouldn't have Colonel Moody and his regiment of soldiers; it would have Brian Canfield and his leadership team.

The Colony of British Columbia was proclaimed at Fort Langley in 1858, and in the ensuing months, Colonel Moody, the ranking commander in the area, selected a site to serve as the capital. For a short time, the growing town was called Queensborough, but Queen Victoria herself ordered the name be changed to New Westminster.

The local economy grew rapidly, thanks to both the gold fields and the expanding fishing and timber industries. Miners poured into the region to stake their claims. Few found wealth, but the support industries around them did—hotels, brothels, restaurants, general stores, and dry goods providers were the real beneficiaries. When the colonies of British Columbia and Vancouver Island were united in 1866, New Westminster was declared the capital.

A rapidly expanding agriculture industry attracted newcomers to the Fraser River region, and lumber production became a mainstay. The fisheries were unequalled in production volume. Since the Fraser River provided unlimited hydropower and a way to transport manufactured goods, factories and mills grew up along its banks.

In 1867, with Confederation, the country of Canada came into being. Five years later, the Colony of British Columbia became a province. As part of the Confederation agreement, the federal government extended the Canadian Pacific Railway's westbound line all the way west, a project that was completed in 1885. The new line allowed industrial goods to be loaded at New Westminster's port and transported across Canada and beyond. New Westminster's downtown district along Columbia Street expanded, with new businesses arriving weekly to serve the growing riverside town. In 1898, a fire roared through the central business district, reducing most of it to rubble. Within a few years, however, the downtown had been rebuilt, and once again economic growth gained a foothold.

Industries diversified, and over the next several decades, Columbia

Street, nicknamed "the Golden Mile" by local business leaders, boasted a diversity of enterprises, including paper mills, lumber mills, textile manufacturers, shipping companies, and businesses that supported the shrinking mining industry.

Like most towns with water access, New Westminster became prosperous, and it generated hundreds of

blue-collar jobs for hard-working residents.

One of the men who benefited from this situation was Orra Wells Canfield. He and his wife, Effie, were residents of New Westminster. Effie, born in Chilliwack in 1916, had moved to New West with her mother and siblings upon the death of her father in 1920. Orra was born close by and,

A photo of Effie and Orra Canfield, Brian's parents, taken in 1962.

own tools from pieces of scrounged wood and metal. He passed this skill on to his son, Brian, who was born on July 9, 1938.

Brian Canfield was an only child, doted on by his parents. New Westminster was a tight and congenial blue-collar community. People helped each other, especially during the lean years of World War II, and that aspect of the local culture was not lost on young Brian. Nor, it turned out, was the industrial nature of the town, which interested the boy. His innate fascination with mechanics, engineering, and the inner workings of complex industrial machinery made him well suited for a future career in a highly technical industry.

The Canfield family lived on Kelly Street for all of Brian's childhood. Effie offered piano lessons in their home and served as the church organist every Sunday. She taught Brian to play the piano, and he became good at it; while he doesn't play often today, he still has his mother's piano in his home. When the time came for Orra and Effie to retire, they moved to a home on Laurel Street.

when he was old enough, found work in a lumber mill in the Maillardville area of Coquitlam, adjacent to New Westminster. He was a steamfitter, which was a highly desirable position in the days when steam was the principal power source for industry. Orra was also handy, making many of his

As Brian himself recalls, he was a typical rambunctious boy. He and his best friend, Larry Pertch, who lived across the street, explored the extensive bush that surrounded New Westminster, building forts and tree houses, and fishing in Brunette Creek. They played marbles and climbed trees, and in the fall they would gather horse chestnuts to play conkers. Sometimes they would hang around at the Canfield home; Pertch remembers that they had to be on their toes at all times because Brian's mother was a stickler for etiquette. Most of the time, however, they played outside until they heard the telltale whistle from one of the moms, signalling that it was time to come in and get washed up for supper.

Brian's paternal grandfather was a school principal in New Westminster who retired in 1938, the year Brian was born. By the time Brian and his friends went through school, his grandfather had become a substitute teacher. He sometimes taught Brian's classes.

There were five movie theatres in the town of 32,000 people, and Brian and his friends often headed off to watch Tom Mix, Gene Autry, and Wyatt Earp tame the Old West. As they got older they frequented the

*Three genera-
tions of Canfields,
1957. From the
left, Brian; his
father, Orra; and
his grandfather,
Francis.*

White Spot, the famous local drive-in complete with carhops on roller skates.

Brian attended Lester Pearson High School. There were about three hundred kids in his grade-twelve class, and those who knew Brian remember him as friendly, gracious, respectful, polite, and honest. According to childhood friend Patti Armstrong, Brian was always prepared—a key Boy Scout attribute. On test days, he was awake by 5 AM studying and was usually the first person in the classroom—largely because he was ill-prepared, according to Brian. Later, at BC Tel and TELUS, colleagues would make a game out of trying to get to meetings before Brian. They rarely succeeded.

Brian Canfield was not a particularly competitive kid; he played a little bit of lacrosse, but just for fun. He wasn't interested in earning letters for his school sweater. Although he would receive many accolades over the course of his career, the trappings of personal recognition always meant little to him.

Brian did have an Achilles' heel, however: he bored easily. He was bright, but after doing something for a period he would grow restless and move on to the next thing that caught his attention. He had the aptitude to excel academically, but school didn't challenge him. "The thing is," Brian says, "I was a pretty poor student. It wasn't that I didn't have the ability to perform, or that I wasn't capable, or that it didn't turn me on; at the time, I just didn't click in school." By the time he reached the end of grade twelve, he had missed so many classes that he didn't have enough credits to graduate. He went through the motions on the day of the ceremony, but he didn't complete high school with his peers. He wasn't overly concerned about the fact; he had no idea

what he wanted to do with his life, and he knew that he could always go back to finish school at some later point, which he did—years later. But thanks to an event he attended just before the end of his grade-twelve year, his life took a propitious turn.

Brian left high school in 1956, a period when the global economy was strong and corporations were thriving. Companies were hiring millions of people to support that growth. Furthermore, what would become the modern high-tech industry was starting to emerge.

In 1956, technology was a vague concept with little significance to the average person. Although primitive by contemporary standards, the technologies of the time were nonetheless changing the face of business. Early that year, the Transistorized Experimental computer zero (TX-0) was demonstrated at the Massachusetts Institute of Technology. John Bardeen, Walter Brattain, and William

Shockley received the 1956 Nobel Prize in Physics for developing the solid-state transistor. On September 13, 1956, IBM Corporation released the 305 RAMAC (Random Access Method of Accounting and Control), the first computer in the world with a hard drive. Weighing well over nine hundred kilograms, its fifty sixty-centimetre-diameter platters were capable of storing five megabytes of data—roughly the size of a single iTunes song. That same year,

IBM announced the programming language FORTRAN, and on September 25, the TAT-1 transatlantic telephone cable was inaugurated between Europe and North America. It was capable of carrying 36 simultaneous telephone calls. (A single optical fibre today can carry over 300,000.) The cable was inaugurated by a call from the chairman of AT&T over a dual connection between London and Montreal, and London and New York.

Because of all this inventive effort during the 1950s, craft jobs and craft skills were in high demand. Highly technical industries like those producing and operating radios, televisions, telephones, and computers required a skilled labour force to support the growing base of customers those industries attracted. Many of these technical employees came from the ranks of the military, enlisted people who had been trained in electronics and were seeking jobs after being discharged. But many companies also conducted job fairs at college campuses and high schools—including Lester Pearson High School in New West.

"One day toward the end of the school year," Brian remembers, "we had a sort of a job fair at the high school. A couple of companies came out to talk about themselves—what they did, how important they were to the community, that kind of thing. The companies were BC Tel and IBM.

Lester Pearson High School, which Brian Canfield attended, was completed in 1955.

So I listened to both of their presentations and decided to apply for a job with BC Tel. More than anything else, I decided to go with the telephone company because I was familiar and comfortable with them. Everybody knew BC Tel's green trucks; they were always driving around the neighbourhood. Plus, I knew people who worked for them, so I was comfortable with the idea of going to work for the phone company."

He chuckles before continuing. "The reason I didn't consider IBM is because I honestly didn't know what IBM was. I wasn't much of a student when I was in high school, and as a result of that I spent a lot of time in the principal's office. The principal had a clock on the wall of his office— one of those big, white, commercial

things—and apparently it had been a gift from IBM, because it had their three-letter logo on the face. Well, I may not have known what kind of a career I wanted at that point in my life, but I sure as heck knew that I didn't want to go to work for a clockmaker! The telephone company seemed a lot more interesting, so I interviewed with them."

Applying for a position with BC Tel in those days involved a series of hurdles: a job interview; an exam that tested reading skills, comprehension abilities, mental dexterity, and mathematical prowess; and a medical examination.

Within TELUS, the story is told— correctly—that Brian Canfield finished high school on Tuesday and began what would become a fifty-eight-year career with TELUS on Thursday. Brian confirms that version of events: "After I did my interview on that Tuesday, I had to write this little exam. It wasn't too complicated, and I passed. I came into town the next day for my company physical—they required them back then. The problem was that I

didn't really know my way around Vancouver. I was from New Westminster, after all, twelve miles away, so by the time I got to the building I was already late, and on top of that I couldn't find a parking place. I waited a few minutes for the elevator, and when it didn't come I ran up eight flights of stairs to get to the medical offices.

"When I ran in, I was red-faced and out of breath, and the first thing they did was take my blood pressure. The doctor read the results and said, 'This is pretty high—I think we'll have to let some of this out.' He was joking, of course, but I didn't know that. He took out a syringe and drew blood for a blood test, and I was so naive that I sat there wondering how much blood he was going to have to take out before he'd be able to get a normal reading."

The next day, Brian Canfield started work as an apprentice equipment installer for the British Columbia Telephone Company.

FACING:
*Direct dialing
was such a novelty
when it became
available that
people lined up to
make calls that
didn't require an
operator.*

The Telephone Industry in 1956

From its beginnings in the late 1870s, when Alexander Graham Bell, Elisha Gray, Thomas Edison, and a collection of lesser-known but no less important innovators gave the world the "speaking telegraph," the telephone industry evolved and grew, with the rules of engagement set almost universally by the American Telephone and Telegraph Company, better known as AT&T. Managed and operated like a military entity, AT&T almost singlehandedly designed and created the largest, most complex machine ever built: the global telephone network.

AT&T was the ultimate vertically integrated company. By 1940, it controlled virtually the entire North American telephone market, including equipment and network design, manufacturing, sales, maintenance, repair, research and development, local calling and long distance. In addition to covering the United States, AT&T had operations in Canada and the Caribbean. AT&T provided everything—phones, circuits, switches, and calling plans. Was it possible for a customer to buy a phone from another company and use it on the AT&T network? Sure—as long as the customer didn't mind buying the phone, giving it to AT&T, paying the company a "rewiring" charge, and then forking over a monthly lease fee for the right to use the customer's own phone to make calls. In 1949, the U.S. Department of Justice filed suit to break up the monopoly, or at least to make it harder for AT&T to behave like one.

The result of this legal challenge was an agreement known as the Consent Decree of 1956, so-called because AT&T "consented" (in reality, it had no choice in the matter) to be restructured by the U.S. government. As part of the agreement, AT&T's control over the market was reduced to 85 per cent. The company was restricted on the number of government contracts it was allowed to bid on; it was prohibited from entering the new and exciting computer industry, and it was put on notice to divest itself of its Canadian and Caribbean operations. This included Bell Canada and Northern Electric, the manufacturing firm that ultimately became Nortel Networks.

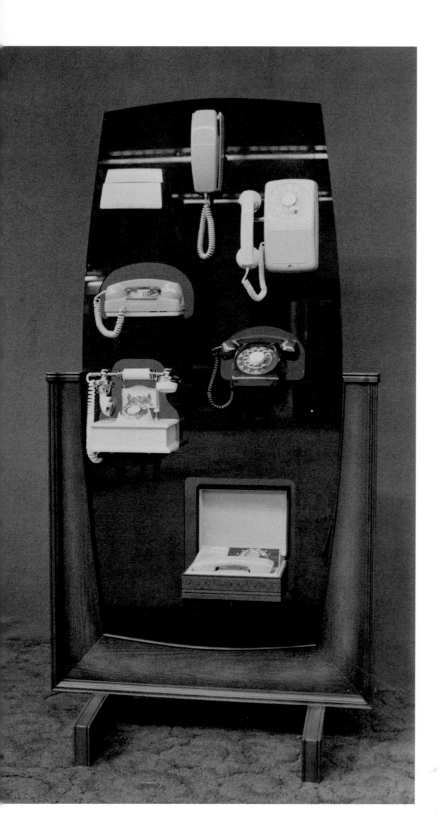

The Consent Decree of 1956, signed into law the year Brian Canfield started his career with BC Tel, set the stage for the ultimate divestiture and breakup of AT&T.

This was the business that Brian Canfield stepped into. The stage had been set for a competitive Canadian telephone industry, but it wasn't yet there. BC Tel, like all telephone companies at the time, operated as a benevolent monopoly, providing its customers with comprehensive communications capabilities. To do that, it needed human resources—lots of them. BC Tel's organization chart, like that of any telephone company at the time, looked like a pyramid, narrow at the top and massively wide at the bottom, reflecting the relative numbers of executives, managers, and technicians required for the company to operate effectively.

The year Brian joined the company also saw numerous technological and organizational innovations. As he recalls, "Phone companies were changing all their technology from 'Number, please' to dial phones." By 1956, automatic direct dialing was available to some Canadians. The first transatlantic telephone cable was laid between the U.K. and Newfoundland in 1956, and that September, Winnipeg brought same-day television programming from CBC TV to its citizenry for the first time when it connected to Trans-Canada Telephone System's microwave radio relay system via Manitoba Telecom Services.

Customers had a single choice for their telephone services. Reminiscent of Henry Ford's famous words, customers could have any colour of phone they wanted, as long as it was black. There was some variation: you could have a Model 40 for your desk or a Model 50 for your wall.

The Canadian Industry

The telephone originally made its way into Canada in 1878, when the Montreal Telegraph Company and the Dominion Telegraph Company inaugurated competitive telephone service in Ottawa, Montreal, Quebec City, St. John's, and a handful of other eastern cities. After pummelling each other for two years in a no-win battle

over price, the two companies turned their assets over to the newly incorporated Bell Telephone Company, which had just received its charter of operations from the federal government.

Jules-André Brillant, who grew up in the Assemetquagan Mission (now Routhierville) in Quebec's Matapedia Valley, joined the Compagnie d'électricité d'Amqui in 1911, and in 1913, at age twenty-five, he began an aggressive and well-planned strategy of growth. In 1922, he acquired the Grand Metis Falls near Rimouski and constructed hydroelectric facilities there. Brillant and his partners founded the Compagnie de Pouvoir du Bas-Saint-Laurent and in 1927 acquired the Compagnie de Téléphone National, which in 1955 became Québec-Téléphone. Brillant's masterfully executed strategy of growth and acquisition provided an economic stimulus to the country and established a successful firm that would one day be part of TELUS.

Bell had also set itself up to provide phone service in several cities from Winnipeg westward. Once Bell had made it as far west as Alberta, company strategists decided that although Calgary was a promising site for phone service, Edmonton was too small to be worth its while.

This slight was not lost on the citizens of Edmonton, and they had their chance for payback when Alex Taylor, a former employee of the Dominion Telegraph and Signal Service, took an interest in the affair. Taylor was one of the founders of the city; he was also the town's first telegraph operator, meteorologist, timekeeper, and self-described lightning manipulator. Frustrated by Bell's decision, Taylor proposed that Edmonton connects itself with the town of St. Albert, fourteen kilometres away, via a homegrown telephone system. He purchased two beautiful telephones crafted from Spanish mahogany and asked storeowner H.W. McKenney, a well-known retailer in St. Albert, to host the other end of the telephone line at his shop.

By 1893, Edmonton had grown large enough to require legitimate infrastructure. Taylor's business empire, which had grown steadily, stepped in and began to offer both electricity and telephone service to the town. Soon, the Edmonton District Telephone Company was also offering service in St. Albert, Jasper Place, Fort Saskatchewan, and Leduc.

When Bell Telephone advanced on Edmonton, looking to maintain its monopoly, Taylor responded by establishing a relationship with the Canadian Pacific Railway for long-distance service. It was something of a hollow victory—Bell already had an agreement to run facilities along the railroad right-of-way and to also supply telephones. But the battle was far from over. Frank Oliver, publisher of the *Edmonton Bulletin* newspaper and a local member of Parliament, campaigned successfully to change the law that granted Bell an exclusive position with the railroad. By 1904, Edmonton was officially a city, and the Edmonton District Telephone Company had become a municipal holding. On the provincial level, Alberta Government Telephones (AGT) started its life in 1906, after a handful of acquisitions that included Bell's regional assets in 1908.

Nov 31 ,1900

M. Alexner & Co.
To Vernon & Nelson Telephone Company, Dr.

Date.	To Whom.	Place.	From Whom.	Place.	Charge.
Oct 6	J. S. Griffin	Nelson	No 48	Ross	40
11	Wash. Br. Lime Co	Spokane	"	"	50
15	Griffin	Nelson	"	"	20
20	Jordan	Trail	"	"	10
					$1 20

BC Tel's Beginnings

British Columbia's communications story begins at the dawn of the twentieth century. William Farrell, born in Ireland, moved to Vancouver in 1891 to assume the position of general manager of the Yorkshire and Canadian Trust Ltd., with full responsibilities for dealings in British Columbia.

The first telephones in the province had been installed on Vancouver Island in 1878, and since then small private exchanges had been popping up throughout the province. Farrell wasted no time jumping on the bandwagon, making a substantial investment in the recently formed New Westminster and Burrard Inlet Telephone Company. In short order he had arranged the acquisition of a handful of regional carriers, including the Victoria and Esquimalt Telephone Company. On July 5, 1904, the assemblage of small companies was incorporated as the BC Telephone Company Limited. Twelve years later, the company received a federal charter and dropped the "Limited" from its name.

In 1929, a charter established a BC Tel subsidiary called the North-West Telephone Company. Created to offer radiotelephone service to the unreachable areas of the province, the company soon offered service to Powell River from Campbell River across the Strait of Georgia, a major technological accomplishment for the time.

Farrell led the BC Telephone Company for the first twenty years of its existence, creating frameworks for growth and strong operating models. In 1926, Theodore Gary and Company, operating under the auspices of the Anglo-Canadian Telephone Company, acquired a large interest. Under the U.S.-based Anglo-Canadian, the BC Telephone Company prospered and grew, and in 1955, American General Telephone & Electric Corporation (GTE) became the 50.2 per cent majority owner of BC Tel when its parent company, Theodore Gary and

Company, merged with the BC Telephone Company. This would set the stage for some remarkable changes in the years ahead.

Regulation Rears Its Head

In 1903, following Frank Oliver and Alex Taylor's successful campaign to shine unfavourable light on Bell's hegemonic practices, Bell Canada had found itself under growing government scrutiny and ultimately under the control of the newly signed Railway Act of 1903 as a "common carrier," resulting in a power shift that required (among other things) that all proposed rate changes be approved by the Board of Railway Commissioners for Canada. This set the stage for the long-term relationship between all service providers in the country and the various regulatory agencies that would culminate in 1968 in the formation of the Canadian Radio-Television Commission (CRTC). Simultaneously, technological advances continued apace. In 1916, Montreal was connected electronically to Vancouver for the first time. Telephone calls were now possible between Canada's east and west, although the calls were routed in a roundabout way: because the infrastructure across the Prairies was not yet complete, calls were routed from Montreal to Buffalo, then to Chicago, to Omaha, to Salt Lake City, to Portland, and finally up and across the border to Vancouver.

In 1924, direct dialing for local calls was offered in Toronto for the first time. Armies of telephone company employees hit the streets to notify people about the change (they were no longer required to call the operator to place a call) and to show them how to use this newfangled contraption that now had a dial. By 1956, the year Brian Canfield joined BC Tel, Canadians right across the country could place long-distance calls without assistance from an operator. Two years later, on June 18, 1958, the sixty-five-hundred-kilometre trans-Canada microwave network was completed. Carrying telephone calls, data, and television signals, it connected the country and made possible, for the first time, the nationwide broadcast of *Hockey Night in Canada*.

All of this technological, regulatory, and organizational innovation predated Brian Canfield's first job with BC Tel—indeed, much of it happened before he was born. These changes would ultimately provide the basis for his creation of TELUS. For the time being, however, Brian was content simply to be embarking on a new phase of his young life: his entry into the working world.

CHAPTER 2

RANK
AND FILE

WHEN HE BEGAN his career at BC Tel as an apprentice equipment installer, Brian Canfield had a salary of $8.15 a day. Darren Entwistle would later joke that Brian offered him the same entry-level salary in 2000, when Entwistle became the new TELUS CEO. Brian was part of a technological army that was bringing telephone services to the far reaches of the province, a period he remembers fondly. During his early years at BC Tel, he developed a keen awareness of the pivotal role technology can play in a company when it is wielded properly. At the same time, he recognized that technology achieves its greatest value when the people deploying it are informed, aware, and committed to the task. This relationship would inform every decision Brian made throughout his long career.

The Shops: Apprentice Equipment Installer

Brian's first job was in a facility called the Shops. At that time, customers didn't own their phones—the telephone company did. When a customer moved into a new house and ordered phone service, BC Tel would dispatch an installer who would see to it that the customer's circuit was electrically

FACING:
Technicians such as this one, here working in an early step-by-step office, were the backbone of the electromechanical switching environment.

21

connected and would also connect the phone, which was hardwired into the wall. Getting phone service disconnected involved the opposite process: an installer would arrive, disconnect the circuit, disconnect the customer's phone or phones, and return them to the company. Once returned, the phones were sent to the Shops, where they were disassembled, cleaned, and prepared for delivery to another customer.

"In those days," Brian explains, "telephones were these old black Bakelite things that were extremely heavy. Inside of them you found big electromagnets, and the ringer was a pair of brass bells and a clapper. So for my first job, they sent me over to what they called the Shops, where equipment repair and maintenance were done. It was a metal shop for the most part, but all I did was repair those old Bakelite phones. The phones would arrive on big trays, and I'd take out four or five at a time, remove the backs, take them completely apart, put the parts in a big pile, then take the Bakelite housings over to these big buffing wheels, where I'd clean them up and then reassemble the phones. It wasn't much of a job, but you had to start somewhere, I figured."

That first position Brian held—and those that followed—helped shape his thinking for the long term. Being represented by a union—the Federation of Telephone Workers, later renamed the Telecommunications Workers Union—gave him an appreciation for the verticality of both the company and the telephone industry, an appreciation that would serve him well in later years when he found himself dealing with mergers and acquisitions, and labour issues. Even in that first job he took his responsibilities seriously, giving his all to the work at hand.

BC Tel was organized and run as a top-down hierarchy, with relatively few "generals" at the top, making all the decisions, and vast numbers of "soldiers" carrying out those decisions without questioning them. In Brian's observation, the union operated in similar fashion. Over his years with BC Tel, he would come to believe that the best way to effectively manage a workforce, the *only* way to challenge, engage, and reward dedicated, hard-working employees, was through a rewards-based meritocracy. This became a key theme throughout his career.

The Multiples Shop

After some time at the machine shop, Brian was transferred to an industrial function called the smelter, then on to the Multiples Shop. "In retrospect," Brian says in jest, "I think it was some kind of punishment. My job was to clean tar out of the pole terminal blocks and get them ready for reuse; then I built multiples, which were the complex wired assemblies that

made up the operator positions on the old cord boards. If you can imagine those old positions—each operator sat in front of a board that had a field of dozens and dozens of jacks on it, into which they would plug cables to set up a connection between a calling party and a called party. But each of those jacks had to appear in front of every operator in the office, so these big trunk cables would come up from the basement and be connected to the back side of each operator position.

"It was a terrible job, but I learned a lot about not only technology but people as well."

Every jack that appeared in front of an operator, such as those shown here, represented a customer's telephone line. An operator typically managed about a hundred appearances.

Assembling the cables that interconnected the various elements of operator-assisted telephony was a complex, painstaking task.

The task of wiring the back of the operator service positions was enormously complicated. Every jack appearance—one for each customer—had to be physically wired to every operator position. Here, three technicians wire the back of a board while operators complete calls on the front.

Collision

In those early days, Brian moved around a lot and performed a dizzying array of tasks. He worked in more than thirty locations across British Columbia for BC Tel's wholly owned subsidiary, Canadian Telephone & Supplies Ltd. "The places they sent me were all over the map," Brian explains, "but I didn't stay in any of them for very long. Sometimes it was just an overnight assignment, and the next day I'd be sent somewhere else."

His responsibilities varied somewhat, but all of them revolved around the maintenance, installation, and repair of telephone company assets. The moves presaged a sea change in the industry, and as he moved from job to job, location to location, Brian began to develop a sense of the expanse, complexity, and centrality of the telephone industry. Each new position he was assigned to added another element of comprehension to his growing awareness of BC Tel's role in business and in society at large. He was also learning first-hand about a key technology-driven change that was taking shape: the looming arrival of automatic switching. By the time Brian joined BC Tel, switching—a function performed by operators to connect customers to each other—had been a mainstay of telephone company operations for almost sixty-five years. The arrival of the hardware-based switching function, however, would transform service delivery, as well as Brian's perspective on the company's role.

The telephone industry began with a man by the name of Almon Strowger. Strowger was an undertaker in Kansas City, Missouri, in the late 1890s. He ran a prosperous business there, but over time, he noted a disturbing trend in his trade: customer volume was steadily declining. It wasn't because the death rate in Missouri had gone down; it was because Strowger's primary competitor was married to the town's only

telephone operator. Whenever a call came in for an undertaker from a distraught customer, the operator naturally connected the calling party to her husband.

Strowger set out to correct the injustice by inventing and then building the world's first mechanical switch, which allowed customers to dial the number of the person they wished to call. In 1901, the Automatic Electric Company began to manufacture Strowger switches under a licence from Strowger's company, and in 1908 the two companies merged and began to operate under the Automatic Electric name. GTE later merged with Automatic Electric and turned it into its own wholly owned manufacturing arm.

FACING:
The "cord board," as it was called, was the heart and soul of the telephone company.

LEFT:
Almon Strowger was an undertaker in Missouri who became famous for inventing the world's first telephone company switch. His invention became the step-by-step switch, a technology that Brian Canfield installed for BC Tel early in his career.

ABOVE, FACING:

"The voice of Ma Bell" emanated from the hundreds of operators who worked to deliver service, all day, every day.

RANK AND FILE 29

The conversion was a massive project in both scale and scope. It represented a major investment for BC Tel in a transformative new technology. It required significant organizational changes in terms of operations, maintenance, and technical support. And it created a tectonic shift in human resources. The role of the operator shifted away from the cord board, and skilled technicians were needed to maintain the thousands of moving parts in these new switches.

Brian finished his assignment in Oliver in June 1958. From there he moved on to work in Vancouver and in various locations on Vancouver Island. In 1959, he met Bev, who also worked for BC Tel. They would marry two years later.

"I had married in April 1961," he remembers, "and my wife, Beverley, sure as heck didn't like all the travelling I was doing. It was hard for her: I'd park her in one town, and then I'd move around every second or third night, leaving her alone most of the time. That just wasn't good for married life. So I applied for a transfer into BC Tel proper, as a central-office maintenance person."

Switching technology continued to evolve, and in late 1957, Brian Canfield was deployed to Oliver, British Columbia, as part of the team that installed a complete electromechanical step-by-step office based on the Automatic Electric Strowger switch. They installed the main distribution frame, the switch.

FACING:
The main distribution frame, or MDF, *supported the miles and miles of wire that interconnected the vastly intricate telephone-company central office. It also served as the interconnection point between the customer's line and the operator— later, the switch.*

LEFT:
Beverley and Brian on their wedding day.

Brian was accepted for the position and sent to the Whalley office in the town centre of Surrey in the spring of 1962. There he remained until 1966, learning the intricacies of central office operations, when he left for Engineering. By this time, he and Bev had begun to have children. Their son Brian had arrived on December 3, 1963, and the lifestyle Brian's work required was beginning to take its toll.

The Central Office

Today, the switches in a telephone company's central office are large, highly sophisticated computers. But the electromechanical switches of the 1950s and 1960s had thousands upon thousands of moving parts—finely tuned actuators and selectors and relays that had to be routinely adjusted, polished, and burnished to ensure they remained within operating tolerances. This was the environment into which Brian transferred.

"That was the end of the Earth," he says, shaking his head. "The amount of work required to keep one of those offices operating around the clock was astounding. We would adjust equipment, install cable, run maintenance checks, and perform dozens of other tasks, at which point we'd start over—go back to the beginning and do it all again. That was the nature of the work. It was highly repetitive and more than a little bit boring. But it had to be done. Postpone maintenance on the moving parts of that old switching equipment for more than a few days and things stopped working."

Brian became increasingly frustrated by the work. He was good at it, and he was learning and gaining experience, but he realized that something was missing: intellectual challenge. He discussed his frustration with his wife. Beverley had the answer, he recalls: " 'You have to go back to school.' " So that's what he did, enrolling at the British Columbia Institute of Technology.

BCIT, formerly BC Vocational School, offered programs based on the model created by City and Guilds of London Institute. The U.K.-based vocational institution provides more than five hundred professional qualifications under the auspices of eighty-five hundred colleges and training providers in more than eighty countries. The programs are so popular—and effective—that two million students around the world still enter the qualification process annually, in such fields as professional engineering, technology, and management.

In 1965, Brian enrolled in BCIT's semester-based program, working all day and taking classes at night. It was an intensive four-year business curriculum, and after completing the first year he accepted a new position at BC Tel in traffic engineering. The job offered a guaranteed level of base pay as well as annual increases—a compelling prospect for someone with a young family.

Over the next few years, Brian balanced school, work, and his increasingly busy personal life. His son Bruce was born on November 17, 1965, adding another mouth to feed. And on top of learning to be a parent, Brian found himself in the most challenging position he had experienced so far at BC Tel.

Technology was expanding, the industry was evolving, and competition was peeking over the horizon. Telecommunications was becoming a mature business, and the pace of change was increasing. But the fun was just beginning. Brian Canfield was in a race, but it wasn't a sprint, and he knew it: it was a marathon. The hard work was still ahead, and there was much to be done.

CHAPTER 3

THE FORMATIVE YEARS

FROM 1966 UNTIL 1968, working in the centrally important field of traffic engineering, Brian began to forge his own career-long approach to problem solving, effective management and leadership.

Traffic engineering is one of the most critical and complicated functions performed by telephone companies. It is the main mechanism by which network providers determine how much capital outlay they must incur to guarantee optimal levels of service for their customers. The function lies at the sensitive balance point between customer service and cost effectiveness.

From his new vantage point, Brian soon realized that superior customer service derived from a combination of elements. Customer satisfaction was a result of a positive customer experience, and that positive experience was the result of a well-designed network. Good network design needed to take into account such factors as cost, traffic volume, human behaviour, technological capability, design capacity, Erlang Theory (a technique for mathematically modelling the behaviour of networks under load), and business strategy. This evolution in Brian's thinking would shape the way he saw his company's

FACING:
The responsibility of maintaining the equipment that supported networks like CONUS Autovon could be challenging—to say the least. Microwave towers like this one had to be maintained, even in the worst conditions.

35

role for the rest of his career—so much so that, based on his recommendation, TELUS Human Resources executive Josh Blair concluded that a clear understanding of engineering economics was crucial to the business and supported the creation of the company's own network engineering and economics courses.

Into the Management Machine

In 1968, Brian was promoted to management. His first assignment was supporting a U.S. military voice network that came to be known as CONUS Autovon (Continental United States Automated Voice Network). Designed to support what is now known as the North American Aerospace Defense Command, the system had been put into service in June 1966.

CONUS Autovon was a complex network, with a complex mission, that comprised buried carrier cable, microwave facilities, open wire, and optical fibre. As a consequence, its operation and management were equally challenging. It's no surprise, then, that Brian's role there was in

network management, the function that oversees the complex operation of the network itself. Network management extends tentacles into every facet of a telephone company, so it was an ideal—albeit challenging— place for him to develop his understanding of network operations.

One of the customers Brian supported in his new position was a branch of the Canadian military. "Even though I wasn't really working on electronics," Brian recalls, "there were some things I realized I needed to know if I was going to be good at my job. The military operated some simple computers, so I felt it was important for me to know something about them.

"But here was the problem. It was the late 1960s, and there just wasn't much out there in the way of computer training. The other thing was that there weren't any compilers around yet—everything was written in the zeroes and ones of machine language. So that's how I learned programming. I taught myself machine language: exclusive and inclusive ORs, and all that wonderful stuff. If the program stopped someplace, you had to go in with an oscilloscope and figure out where the flip-flops were to figure out what word it had failed on."

Brian haunted libraries, bookstores, and the university, ultimately assembling a collection of books and reference materials from which to teach himself. He realized that, given the direction the industry was taking, a background in information technology would serve him well. He asked BCIT if it would be possible for him to enroll in the second year of a two-year FORTRAN programming course (bypassing the first year), and it agreed. He enrolled, and passed. The combination of what he learned in the program and the skills he taught himself gave him the background he needed to operate credibly in the emerging "transition zone" between telephony and IT. Brian makes his accomplishment sound easy, but by any measure, this was an extraordinary achievement. Even computer science students who spend multiple semesters studying machine language rarely get beyond a basic, academic understanding of its inner

workings. Brian went well beyond that level, achieving a functional and diagnostic mastery of the technology, even though it wasn't even close to being part of his job description. This became a central part of his professional character. Indeed, many of his peers over the years would express "friendly frustration" that no matter how hard they worked to master a particular area of the business, Brian would challenge them with questions that indicated his knowledge of the subject exceeded their own.

The more time Brian spent with his military client, the more aware he became that a well-managed network leads to higher levels of customer satisfaction. In the case of this particular customer, the traffic the network carried was more than routinely important. The lessons Brian had learned at Haney Radio, supporting CONUS Autovon, proved helpful to him in his new management role. When NASA engineers described the space shuttle as "twenty million individual parts flying in close formation," they could well have been describing a modern telecommunications network.

Brian understood this all too well, and he was one of the first people to deliberately focus on network management as a dedicated function at BC Tel. He shared his understanding of the centralized management model with offices throughout the province that were in the process of turning up similarly complex networks. At every turn, he preached the cost-versus-benefit mantra.

In the business world, the quality of telephone service was fast becoming a differentiator in a competitive market. Hotels, for example, which typically had a phone or two in the lobby for guests to use if they needed to make a call, suddenly experienced growing demand for in-room telephones. It was a challenge that increased the cost and complexity of running a hotel. There was simply no system available that would allow the hotel to invoice, in real time, individual line usage on a room-by-room basis. Similarly, pay telephones were incapable of collecting toll charges, which dramatically limited their revenue potential. A new system was required, one that would make possible more complex data collection and analysis.

TSPS Arrives

The problem was resolved with the arrival of a new computerized system called the Traffic Service Position System, or TSPS. Brian Canfield was promoted to second-level manager in the early 1970s, at about the time TSPS found its way into the company, and he was part of the team that brought the system into BC Tel and got it working. BC Tel expected to see immediate benefits, because there were dozens of hotels in Vancouver. Brian became the front man

for that effort, visiting hotel after hotel to explain and demonstrate what TSPS could do for it: if the hotel installed a direct link to the service, BC Tel could give it the response it needed to do real-time complex billing. The telephone industry was still a monopoly, but Brian wasn't selling only services. He was selling BC Tel and the role it could play in a new and compelling future for the customers it represented.

TSPS was a complicated system: it provided a temporary switched connection to an operator who handled calls requiring assistance, such as person-to-person calls, collect calls, and calls billed to a third party. TSPS also offered a feature called the Hotel Billing Information System (HOBIS),

*Brian and Bev
with their children.*

which made it possible to automatically bill long-distance calls made from guest rooms in near real time. The hotels that subscribed to this service had dedicated Teletype data circuits to transport the information required. Needless to say, this made customers in the hospitality industry extremely happy—not to mention hotel guests. The new system was complex and somewhat daunting, but Brian did the same thing he'd done with machine language: he dug into the bowels of TSPS and made sure

that he understood it from top to bottom.

"I had a lot of fun trying to apply that kind of technology and to look for opportunities to put it into use," he says. "TSPS was modern technology at the time, although I laugh now when I think about it. It had these Nixie tube displays that were always failing, and it used Automatic Electric equipment. Even though the original design came out of Bell Labs and was based on transistor technology, in many ways it was, even then, a bit primitive. But here's the thing: I was fascinated by that technology. It got me hooked."

On the human side, Brian also understood something important. He explained to potential customers how the system worked and what benefits it would bring them, but he also assured them that BC Tel would handle the technology. The technical details would never have to be the customer's concern: that was part of the service BC Tel delivered. Brian's instincts about the relationship between the company and the customer would always serve him well.

From Telephones to IT

Brian continued to develop his technical skills as the 1960s came to a close, and he and Bev heralded the beginning of the new decade with the arrival of their daughter, Nancy, on February 1, 1970.

In 1976, he accepted a position in what would ultimately become BC Tel's information technology organization, known at the time as Management Information Systems, or MIS. He was fascinated by this new world of computers and data processing, reading everything he could find about the technology, and taking every opportunity to interact with it. He'd hoped he'd have the opportunity in his new job to actually work with the technology, but it was not to be. His position was a purely administrative one that offered little in the way of professional challenge.

So, later that year, Brian left MIS and accepted a position—actually, he accepted a demotion—with the team that was implementing the Directory Assistance Information System, whimsically known as DAISY. Up

until then, directory assistance had been a manual function requiring hundreds of operators, who consulted paper records. The system was extremely costly and slow, and as the volume of directory assistance calls increased, Operator Services had more and more difficulty handling the load. Brian found DAISY exciting at first. When operational, it would mechanize the directory assistance function so that operators could get immediate electronic access to directory information. Once the system

Always quick to identify a market, BC Tel zeroed in on the teenager's demand for a phone of her own.

*"Concept products"
like this space-
age telephone
booth reflected the
world's mania for
technology in the
1960s.*

LEFT:
*Telephones and
Telesat—a per-
fect combination
in this 1960s
campaign, high-
lighting the latest
and greatest in
communications
technology.*

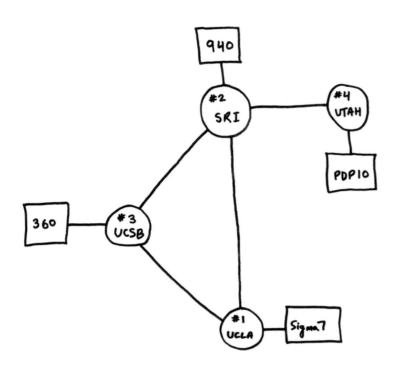

"I'd asked them, 'Why me? I don't know anything about this,'" Brian recalls. "They told me maybe that was a good thing—that by bringing in somebody who had never done it before we might get different—meaning better—results."

A Technological Turning Point

The time frame for this particular transition in Brian Canfield's career is important. The 1980s were just around the corner, and massive changes had taken effect in the technology sector in the preceding decade and a half. In 1969, ARPANET, the precursor of the modern Internet, went online for the first time. A year later, Intel announced the world's first commercially available dynamic random access memory (DRAM) chip, the Intel 1103. Up until that time, computer memory had been stored on either tiny ferrite rings on fine wires, which could be individually charged to represent a zero or a one, or on magnetic tape, which was extremely slow and easy to damage. Solid-state memory was a game changer.

was up and running, and had been debugged, however, he lost interest. The challenge was gone; it was time to turn his talents elsewhere.

Because of his success with the DAISY project, Brian was promoted to third-level management, and shortly thereafter, in 1978, he received a call, asking if he would be interested in an assignment with BC Tel's Supplies, Transportation and Building division. He accepted and soon found himself responsible for the supply chain—all the inventory, purchasing, and support functions related to the day-to-day care and feeding of the company's far-flung operations. The job was radically different from anything he had done before: an appealing proposition, given his penchant for learning.

In 1971, Intel had announced the 4004 microprocessor, the world's first computer-on-a-chip. The Ethernet arrived from Xerox in 1973, heralding the beginning of the local area network and the accelerating use of small-scale computers. This sequence of events would revolutionize the office environment. The combination of high-speed, low-cost, massively scalable local area networks and computer chips meant a departure for most businesses, away from the centralized, mainframe-based computer and toward the PC. Then, in 1975, magic happened with the announcement of the MITS Altair, designed around the Intel 8080 microprocessor. It ran a BASIC operating system developed by Bill Gates and Paul Allen, who cofounded Microsoft. MITS was Microsoft's first customer.

The Altair was a hobbyist's machine, a kit computer, not really designed for business. But things shifted in 1976 and 1977 when a little-known company from California called Apple Computer released the Apple I and II, Commodore released the VIC-20, and Radio Shack came out with the TRS-80.

All of these machines found their way into the business world, but there was very little application software written that would run on them. That changed in 1978 when VisiCalc arrived, bringing a rudimentary spreadsheet to the personal computing domain. In 1979 came WordStar, making word processing widely available. Then, in 1981, *everything* changed: IBM released its MS-DOS-based personal computer, specifically aimed at the business community.

The Business Services Revolution Begins

The revolution wasn't limited to the technology sphere. The culture of business was changing too, and radically. In 1979, Michael Porter of Harvard University published his seminal work on the five forces of competitive advantage, a paper that would change the way businesses thought about their relationships with customers, suppliers, and competitors. In 1982, Tom Peters and Robert Waterman,

FACING:
The practice of selling in the days of telephone company monopoly was a bit different from how it is in today's hyper-competitive environment. Here a group of BC Tel sales professionals go through a sales-planning course.

both McKinsey & Company associates, published *In Search of Excellence,* regarded as one of the best business books ever written. It laid out the practices of excellent companies for all to see.

At around the same time, W. Edwards Deming and Malcolm Baldrige made the most of their research into Japan's innovative business practices and brought Total Quality Management to the Western world. They infected the corporate sphere with a feverish commitment to excel. Organizations like Hewlett-Packard, GE, and Apple were lauded for their innovative approaches to productivity, and the seeds were sown for the creation of Xerox PARC, Silicon Valley, the plethora of technology companies that collected in Kanata, and Research Triangle Park.

None of this was lost on Brian Canfield, who dove in with a vengeance, taking advantage of every opportunity to learn about the touch points between business and technology. While working in the Supplies, Transportation and Building (ST&B) division, he learned about a six-week advanced management program

offered by a consortium of universities in Banff, Alberta. "I asked if I could be sponsored to go," he remembers, "and soon I found myself among some very smart people. That was one of the most important pivotal points for me, because I had never been exposed to much in the way of formal thinking about organizational structure, management, leadership, and so on. Up until then, what I did in those areas was purely intuitive. So I attended that program and thoroughly enjoyed it. What an eye-opener." While Brian continued to rely on intuition and a keen sense of human behaviour throughout his career—both hallmarks of good leadership—the program at Banff provided him with a framework to help organize his thinking as a leader. Soon afterward, he left ST&B to accept a position in sales.

Sales

Telecommunications in the early 1980s was still, for the most part, a monopoly. The cost of building a telecommunications network was shockingly high, and no one other than the

incumbent providers had the financial wherewithal or the inclination to build a competing infrastructure. This would change as competing access technologies and new regulatory decisions emerged.

"The good news," Brian explains today, "was that I went into sales at a time when the technology was evolving such that the natural monopoly enjoyed by the telephone company couldn't be enforced, and shouldn't have been. Technology was reaching a point where it was beginning to enable competition. I had responsibility for general sales for the entire province. That was a pretty rewarding position, because a lot of the topics I had studied at the Banff School, things like engineering economics, lent themselves to this new job I found myself in. I was mostly selling PBX systems [small private switches installed on the customer's premises that provided in-building dialing and other features], but thanks to changes in the industry, I was also selling complex voice and data solutions."

LEICH'S

new look

CORDLESS PBX

At that point in time, Brian recalls, customers had a choice: they could buy their own PBX or they could lease one from BC Tel. "I went into sales when people were actually buying PBXs because they could and then regretting the purchase, because once they owned the technology they also had to operate it, which was a very complicated endeavour.

"One story in particular made me change the way I positioned our products with customers. I had gone over to West Vancouver to talk with a lumber broker who had been writing nasty letters to the regulator [the CRTC], telling them that we weren't being responsive to his company's needs. He had gone down to the States and bought his own PBX system. So the way the technology worked in those days was that he had private lines from BC Tel that went over to a switchboard in the United States, and then looped back into Canada.

"In a PBX system, you dial nine to get to an outgoing line, but the customer claimed that it wasn't working—he'd dial the number but couldn't get a connection. So I watched him dial and then I said, 'I'll bet you a bottle of your favourite drink that I can get through every time.' I then proceeded to do exactly that. What he didn't do, you see, was allow time between dialing the nine and then dialing the telephone number that followed. This was an analogue system, which meant it was slow—it needed time to parse the dialed digits.

"So I told him, 'Do this, then wait, then dial.' He was so impressed that he said, 'I want you to take over my maintenance business. I'll get rid of those other guys.' That was a big transition period. The market was becoming competitive; we were leaving rotary dial behind, and digital was on its way in. I learned a lot during that time, mostly about bringing added value to the relationship with customers."

That experience was indicative of the changes soon to consume the telecommunications industry. Most important of all was a nascent reality that was dawning on telecom: the customer was gaining power, and service providers would ignore that at their peril. Brian had also learned a lot about the actions required to keep customers close. At the same time, his profile in the company was rising

as his successes as a leader became increasingly visible.

Refining the Business: Area General Manager

BC Tel was paying close attention to the renaissance that was underway globally in management and leadership, and it took steps to inculcate the new practices within the company. In the early 1980s, then-CEO Gordon MacFarlane—whom Brian remembers fondly for his innovative, no-nonsense approach to moving the business forward—brought in management consultants McKinsey & Company to advise MacFarlane and the board on their strategic approach to the future of BC Tel.

The advisers, Brian recalls, "were a bunch of young MBAs who ran around and interviewed large numbers of employees to develop a sense of who we were and how we thought about the business. One day they got a bunch of us together to talk about the apparent inability of the company to deliver service to the customer. I didn't hold back. I told the people in the room that it wasn't

FACING:
When the Private Branch Exchange (PBX) first came out, it proved to be a revolutionary technology in terms of its ability to redefine customer service—and control.

a service-delivery problem; the problem was a lack of accountability and the fact that proper forecasting wasn't being done. This was all stuff I had learned at Banff. I told them, 'You think everybody works the same way you do, but that's not the case.' The next morning the McKinsey guy was in my office waiting for me. 'You said you could prove it?' he asked. 'So prove it.' Well, I had a lot of notes and such, and so I proved it."

From those class notes, Brian explains, came a series of changes in the company that resulted in, among other things, a restructuring of the business along geographical lines. The company was divided into five physical segments, each managed by an area general manager. One of those managers was Brian; he was promoted to the position in 1983.

"I was the youngest of them," he says, "and was given downtown Vancouver, from the U.S. border all the way up the coast. I had a huge organization—thirty-five hundred people. So I went from having a hundred people to having thirty-five hundred, almost literally overnight. It was a huge step for me. I went from a pay group 7 to a pay group 11, which was a big jump. But with that change in responsibility came a great deal of stress, so much so that it was unrealistic and unfair. As a result, I would never let anyone else make a similar jump after that. It was just too much—it set people up to fail. You have to build up to take on so much responsibility."

Brian had become an insightful manager by this time. Perhaps more importantly, he had also developed an incisive curiosity, which caused him to question long-standing business practices at every turn. Some industry wonks maintain that the telecom industry's greatest gift to the world was the phrase "If it ain't broke, don't fix it." The expression was coined originally in response to people who would "fiddle" with the complex technology that makes a network do what it does, sometimes making it worse. It came to have a broader meaning in the business world, referring to the tendency to ignore problems in the hopes that they will go away, or to stick with business practices so entrenched they are rarely noticed.

Brian Canfield, however, noticed everything, and he questioned at every turn the practices he saw. His response during the McKinsey study of BC Tel was typical. It was based on his fundamental belief that data doesn't lie, and that the most effective response to a problem often lies in that data. Brian was already putting his mark on the company in a big way, and he would continue to do so.

In 1985, Brian was promoted to vice-president of Technical Support for BC Tel. Technical support was structured at the time as a staff function, administered across the organization as a shared service. That kind of structure didn't allow for any appreciable degree of autonomous operation or customization, however—a serious issue for a corporation as large, diversified, and complex as BC Tel.

Centralizing a desired outcome is one thing; centralizing how you arrive at that outcome is something completely different. With all of BC Tel's sub-organizations forced to do things in exactly the same way, even though they were responsible for vastly different functions, the outcome was, predictably, less than ideal. Groups in different functional silos developed homegrown tech-support systems out of necessity, further fragmenting the operations function.

Telecommunications networks are so complex that a problem in one part of the network can have a waterfall effect, cascading through a vast geography as the network attempts to deal with the failure or overload. If the management and monitoring function is dispersed among multiple organizations, it can be extremely difficult to isolate and resolve a problem in a timely fashion. Because he had seen this happen first-hand, Brian made significant changes in BC Tel's network-management operating model. His actions dramatically improved the function's effectiveness and efficiency throughout the company.

Technology was maturing, the telecommunications industry was getting competitive, and customers were starting to appreciate the possibilities that telecom brought to their businesses. Brian Canfield watched these changes with excitement, poised and ready for the next phase of his career.

CHAPTER 4

INTO THE C-SUITE

IN 1988, BRIAN CANFIELD was appointed executive vice-president of Telephone Operations at BC Tel. In that role he managed the day-to-day operations of the company's telephone network, with the goal of ensuring responsible growth for the company's customer base and the revenues that derived from it. He also focused on strategic planning and organizational goal-setting. His interest in the detailed operation of complex machines—which BC Tel clearly was—not to mention his keen interest in network economics, made him an ideal candidate for the position.

Brian shone in his new role, and he continued his dizzyingly rapid progression through the various levels of senior leadership. In 1989, he accepted the position of president and chief operating officer. In 1990, when CEO Gordon MacFarlane retired, Brian was selected to replace him, becoming the seventh president and CEO of BC Tel. His appointment could not have come at a more critical time in the industry, coinciding as it did with the dawn of modern regulation.

FACING:
Brian Canfield in an early executive portrait.

BRIAN CANFIELD
... takes up reins

Canfield to head B.C. Tel

Brian Canfield, a Coquitlam resident, will take over leadership at B.C. Tel.

Canfield, chief operating officer of B.C. Tel, has been named to replace retiring president Gordon MacFarlane who turns 65 next month.

Canfield will become the chief executive officer and president of the company.

Canfield is also the chairman of Coquitlam's 1991 B.C. Summer Games committee.

MacFarlane will remain as chairman of the board of B.C. Tel.

The Origins of Regulation

Telecommunications regulation in Canada began in earnest in 1906, when the Board of Railway Commissioners was tasked with the additional responsibility of regulating the telephone system. Both railroads and telephone companies were massively capital-intensive to build, represented critical infrastructure for the country, and posed the potential for abuse of their monopoly position. Even the terminology used in the two industries was similar. It was no surprise that many of the original designers of large-scale telephone networks had crossed over from the railroad industry.

Because of the cost associated with the build-out of the railroad and telephone networks, both were considered natural monopolies. Once the Board of Railway Commissioners got involved, regulatory decisions that had long governed the railroad industry began to bleed over into telecom. However, the telephone industry in Canada remained remarkably diverse. By 1915, more than fifteen hundred independent telephone companies were operating throughout the country, all in competition with Bell. It was impossible to regulate an industry that was changing so blindingly fast. The technology was in a constant state of reinvention, evolving drastically with each innovation. Customers were lusting for telephones, and competitors were springing up uncontrollably, sometimes establishing storefronts overnight. Regulators ran along behind in a desperate but futile attempt to keep up. Service providers were often hobbled by short-sighted regulatory decrees that served no one.

Government Becomes an Operator

To provide oversight and structure for the burgeoning industry, government stepped in in certain areas and took control, becoming provincial owner-operators of Alberta Government Telephones in 1906, Manitoba Telephone System in 1908, and Saskatchewan Telephone in 1909. But the chant for a nationwide telephone system—and a central authority to govern it—was getting louder.

All of the companies operating across Canada had the same goal: to offer the people of their regions reliable telephone service. The system, however, was fragmented, at least from a national point of view. Local service could easily be delivered under this model, since the provincial carriers had a captive market. Quebec and Ontario were Bell Telephone territory. The Maritimes did their own thing for the most part, with some degree of organizational

and technological help from Bell. Telephone companies in Alberta, Manitoba, and Saskatchewan were government entities, developing along parallel paths. In the west, the British Columbia Telephone Company took a separate path, ultimately becoming the only major Canadian telephone company to be sold (temporarily) to a U.S. firm.

Long distance, however, was another story. A call from Vancouver to Halifax might use the infrastructure of seven companies, which introduced many complexities. How did intermediate carriers get paid for calls they transported but didn't terminate? How should calls be tracked? Whose responsibility was it if a call failed to go through? Who would ensure that technological standards were maintained across different providers' networks? How would the cost of maintaining shared equipment be handled? And how would advertising and marketing campaigns for long-distance service be conducted?

These questions drove regional telephone companies to think long and hard about the need for a national

telephone companies that served British Columbia, Alberta, Saskatchewan, and Manitoba were encouraged to attend. Bell, from the east, was invited as well. After much discussion, the companies agreed to form the Telephone Association of Canada (TAC).

TAC's initial meetings were hosted in 1921 in Vancouver by George Halse, president of the British Columbia Telephone Company. Speaking at the opening meeting, Halse encouraged members to consider the profound value of a seamless telephone system that would span the country.

All long-distance calls within Canada had to be routed at some point through the United States. This was a vexing concern for TAC members. But how to address it? Bringing phone service to small population centres was not economically feasible. And would the railroads, which already operated their own telegraph circuits, be willing to lease those circuits to a potential competitor?

As member companies pondered these questions, regional carriers began to create ad hoc connections

consortium. Thanks to government subsidy, Canada's railroad system was completed "from the eastern shore to the western strand" by 1885 and opened for business in 1886. Similar public funds, however, were not made available to the country's telephone companies.

In October 1920, Manitoba's Minister of Telephones called a meeting in Winnipeg. The leaders of the among themselves. Alberta, Manitoba, and Saskatchewan established interconnections, as did the Maritime companies with Quebec and Ontario. British Columbia companies connected to those in Alberta.

In May 1926, a singular event took place. Using a Canadian Pacific Telegraph facility, Winnipeg announced a connection with Fort William, Ontario. It was the first indication that the Canadian Pacific Railway might be inclined to lease its facilities to a competing telephone company—important news indeed.

The System Advances

On July 1, 1927, Canada held a Diamond Jubilee to celebrate the sixty years since Confederation. An ambitious goal was set: to broadcast the Parliament Hill festivities to all Canadians, using some 16,950 kilometres of telephone facilities and 14,450 kilometres of telegraph facilities, with the circuits cobbled together by the country's telecommunications companies. Broadcast to every radio in the country, the circuit worked flawlessly. There was only one mechanical failure: because of the summer heat, a poorly soldered connection in Ontario became intermittent, threatening to derail the plan. A lineman dispatched to the offending circuit was instructed by his supervisor to stay on the pole and hold up the wire until the broadcast was complete. The broadcast was hugely successful, and it created a vision for Canadians of what could be.

The following year, the TAC asked Bell Telephone to study the feasibility of a trans-Canada toll system. The resulting report was received enthusiastically, and things moved quickly from there. Seven telephone companies, including BC Tel, agreed to formally connect their long-distance facilities, sharing the cost of the required upgrades. A clearinghouse was established for all trans-Canada business. The seven member companies signed a memorandum of understanding that covered operations, management, and revenue-sharing. Because Bell was the most established company, the other member companies adopted Bell's standard

FACING:
During the Diamond Jubilee celebration, a technician like this one was posted atop a pole to ensure the broadcast was not interrupted by a technical failure.

ROUTE OF
Trans-Canada Telephone System
SHOWING TERMINAL & REPEATER POINTS
Scale of Miles
0 50 100   200   300   400   500

This map of the Trans-Canada Telephone System shows its various service points as it makes its way across the country.

FACING:
The CEOs of the provincial companies that made up Telecom Canada and then formed Stentor.

operating procedures for network management, organizational structure, network engineering, call routing, and network maintenance.

BC Tel Restructures

When Trans-Canada Telephone System (TCTS) came into existence, the seven companies had a total combined investment in TCTS of just over $265 million. They enjoyed a combined customer base of 1,166,823 subscribers. Forty-two thousand long-distance calls were placed in 1932, the first full year of the organization's operation, and revenues totalled a whopping $165,490. In the years that followed, three new members joined TCTS, giving the company cross-country coverage. In 1983, the organization changed its name to Telecom Canada.

By the time Brian Canfield became president and CEO of BC Tel in 1990,

he understood the profound impact Telecom Canada had had on the Canadian business landscape, and he was deeply appreciative of the organization's role as the telecom industry adapted to the evolving demands of the marketplace. In his new position, he pursued a major restructuring of BC Tel, forming three core divisions—Business, Small Business and Consumer, and Emerging Business—to more properly reflect a market-centric, customer-focused operating model. Brian and the other members of BC Tel's management team believed the new structure would fully support the company's corporate mission, which was stated as follows: "We make it easy for people to exchange information—anywhere, anytime—by devising imaginative telecommunications solutions that are economic and that exceed customer expectations."

The Stentor Alliance

"The fundamental issue during the period before TELUS came into existence," Brian recalls, "was that we had ten telephone companies in the country that were part of a loosely held consortium called Telecom Canada. Bell was the largest, we [BC Tel] were the second largest, and Alberta [Alberta Government Telephones] was the third. The Maritime companies were the smallest. Under the banner of Telecom Canada, we had put into place an equalization process [for the division of long-distance revenues], a sort of financial clearinghouse. Before that, if you were a nationwide company like the Royal Bank and you bought a telecom service for the entire company, you'd get different pricing in different regions—clearly not a good thing from a customer-service point of view.

"Well, around that time there was a guy named Ted Rogers [co-founder of what would ultimately become Rogers Communications] and another named Bill Stinson, who was the chairman and CEO of Canadian Pacific Railway. They wanted to create their own consortium, a pretty aggressive play, and I realized pretty quickly that we couldn't survive if the bigger companies came in and began to compete, because they had national scope and we were a series of regional and provincial players. Furthermore, our thinking, as a collection of smaller companies, wasn't particularly well aligned. So the first day I became the CEO of BC Tel, I called up Jean Monty, the new CEO of Bell Canada. I told him I believed we had some good ideas about how we could tackle the national-service issue without having to change the ownership model. I knew that if we didn't, we'd get our lunch eaten by [Rogers-owned] Cantel. So he flew out and we talked, and from that conversation we created the alliance that came to be known as Stentor."

The Stentor Alliance, operating as Stentor Canadian Network Management, was formed in 1992. Technologies advanced as well, with the addition of microwave and high-bandwidth, multichannel optical transport systems. With revenues of $13.5 billion, Stentor generated 78 per cent of all Canadian telecommunications services revenues. The alliance soon restructured itself into three functional entities: Stentor Resource Centre, Stentor Canadian Network Management, and Stentor Telecom Policy.

Brian Canfield recalls the early days of Stentor's existence well—and one meeting in particular. "At the annual meeting, I was up there talking about our idea for this new company called Stentor, and out of the audience the guy who used to be the head of our transmission and engineering department said, 'That's the stupidest name for anything I've ever heard.' He asked how we came up with that, and I said, 'You should have seen what was in second place.' Well, that little exchange went public, and soon after that I was interviewed by the media and was asked, 'What was in second place?' And I said, 'Radian.' Puzzled, the press collectively said, 'Huh?' I told them they clearly didn't know their math: 'It's the angle that subtends the length of the arc based on the radius, which I think is about fifty-seven degrees.' The reporter who had initially asked the question said, 'You're right— Stentor is a good name.'

"The name Stentor was chosen because of its etymological roots— in Greek mythology, the herald Stentor is known as 'the voice of communications.' You were supposed to be able to hear Stentor's voice over the din of battle. So that was the name we selected.

"That moment, when we began to look into the future and I saw the potential for a nationwide company that served everyone, was my pivotal moment. As a result of the creation of the Stentor consortium, we were able to develop scale and scope, standard products, standardized marketing, and many other advantages. Basically, we were able to operate as a nationwide service provider yet still keep our individual company identities."

John Wheeler, who was the head of Investor Relations for the company in Alberta during this time, chuckles as he recalls events from the Stentor days. "The CEOs of the member companies would fly all over the place to have meetings," he explains. "And whether they were on a plane, at a meeting, or eating dinner, they would always sit together in a group, except for Brian. He would always go sit with the executive assistants. It drove the other executives crazy, of course, but there was a method to his madness. 'You find out what's really going on that way,' he was fond of saying."

The End of an Era

Brian served as chair of the Stentor Alliance Council of CEOs from 1994 through 1997. Stentor operated until 1998, when its members chose to dissolve the alliance. The decision was based on numerous factors, but the most important was the desire of the Western Canada telephone companies to join forces against Bell, which was making noises about penetrating their territories more aggressively. The western companies also wanted the freedom to act individually to protect themselves against foreign competitors. Furthermore, the structure of the industry in Western Canada was going through changes that made Brian Canfield question the long-term role of Stentor, particularly if membership in the alliance would inhibit his goal of creating a single, world-class carrier to serve the country.

Changes in the marketplace were also creating a sea change in telecom. In 1990, resellers had entered the Canadian telecom market. As a result, Bell and other regulated players began to experience, for the first time, an erosion of market share. In 1992, the CRTC ruled the Canadian long-distance market open to full competition. And if these forces weren't disconcerting enough, the Stentor member companies had never developed their relationship to a level that could be truly seen as strategic; it was far more tactical, and in Brian Canfield's mind was not adequate to face off against the coming challenges of international and multimodal competition.

TELUS Is Born

Canfield had a laser-like vision of what he wanted the future to look like for BC Telephone; that was the easy part. Now he had to turn that vision into reality. He knew that the new entity he envisioned wouldn't be perfect right out of the gate, but he also knew that it could become very, very

good through a process of deliberate, committed, iterative improvements.

The history of today's TELUS reads like a treatise on the calculated balance between prudent risk and sumptuous reward, and it proceeded like a chess game among grand masters. The story began in 1958, when the Alberta Government Telephones Commission was created. The AGT Commission went through several organizational shifts until 1990, when a company named TELUS Alberta was created and became the parent company of Alberta Government Telephones (AGT). The Alberta government's stake in TELUS sold for $870 million. The TELUS Alberta initial public offering raised $896 million and is still the largest IPO in Canadian financial history.

That same year, the Edmonton Telephones Corporation, operating as Ed Tel, was created as a fully separate subsidiary of the City of Edmonton. Five years later, TELUS AGT acquired Ed Tel from the City of Edmonton for $467 million. In 1996, the Ed Tel and AGT brands were officially retired, and the TELUS master brand appeared on the scene.

Big changes were also afoot in British Columbia. Brian Canfield was named chairman and CEO of BC Telephone in 1993, and under the guidance of Canfield and his board of directors, the company reorganized and changed its legal operating name to BC Tel. Five years later, TELUS Alberta and BC Tel announced that they were considering a merger, the first in a series of steps that would lead to the creation of a national carrier. The merger of the two companies created a titan with $6 billion in annual revenue and assets totalling more than $8 billion. And then there was the anticipated growth: TELUS Alberta president George Petty explained in a news conference at the time, "When we talk about growth, we mean a number of things. We mean accelerating the pace at which we expand into fast-growing, new businesses such as advanced data services, voice over the Internet, and electronic commerce. We also mean building upon our existing network infrastructure and, most importantly, expanding our customer base beyond our provincial borders." Analysts saw the potential in the newly

formed company for annual synergies by the third year of $250 million in operating expenses and $115 million in capital expenses, both of which were easily met.

The deal was signed in early 1999, under the guidance of Don Calder, the former CEO of BC Tel, who structured and negotiated the merger between BC Telecom and TELUS.

As Brian recalls, "When BC Tel and TELUS Alberta completed their merger, 55 per cent of the company was owned by BC Tel, and 45 per cent was owned by TELUS AGT. Under Canadian law, a merger can't be outside those percentage parameters—otherwise it isn't a merger, it's a purchase."

Each company offered up negotiators to guide the process of merging the two companies. "During the discussions we managed to resolve everything except for two issues: what the name of the company would be, and where the headquarters would be located," Brian says. "Because we couldn't get anywhere on a name, we decided initially to call the company BCT.TELUS, a combination of the two names. As far as a headquarters was concerned, we decided that we'd have people in both British Columbia and Alberta. That way we could move forward and close the deal. So we went back feeling pretty good about what we'd accomplished, and then realized that they had already changed all of the logos to TELUS over in Alberta. Furthermore, TELUS made sense because it just wouldn't work to have BC Tel go national, so we compromised. Later, we commissioned a brand study to see whether the name had national presence, and in fact it did. So we decided that if the name was going to be TELUS, and since at that point TELUS was a BC-based company, the headquarters would be in BC. That was the deal we crafted. As a result, we came under the laws of BC instead of under Canadian federal law."

Josh Blair, who serves today as TELUS's chief corporate officer and as executive vice-president for TELUS Health and TELUS International, recalls all of this taking place. "During the time that Stentor was breaking up," he explains, "Bell Canada delivered a very clear message: 'Either align with us or be acquired. We're going to be the new Stentor, and we're going national.' You have to understand that Manitoba Telephone System had signed a strategic alliance with Bell. Bell had acquired all of the Atlantic companies. Saskatchewan was still a government entity, so it wasn't relevant; all that was left was BC Tel and TELUS Alberta, and that's when Brian said, 'You know, we don't want to become a satellite office of Bell Canada.'

"So in mid-1998, the merger of BC Tel and TELUS Alberta was announced, and it was consummated in early 1999. The message was delivered that we were going to expand and take on Bell nationally. It was a very gutsy move; in fact, we really had no idea how to do it. But Brian said, 'We're going to bring competition to Canada.' "

Although there was a great deal of market excitement over the merger, the company did encounter some resistance, most notably—and understandably—from the union. The Calgary-based International Brotherhood of Electrical Workers Local 348 represented 6,175 workers at TELUS Alberta, far and away the majority of the workforce at the time. BC Tel's 10,500 union employees were represented by the Telecommunications Workers Union. Because of the pending merger, the Canada Labour Relations Board announced it would mandate a representation election, which would give workers the opportunity to select a single union to represent them after the merger was complete. Needless to say, both unions saw themselves in a pitched battle for survival. Ultimately, the Telecommunications Workers Union prevailed.

In 1999, following six years of nationwide operations, the Stentor Alliance was officially dissolved. Cellular telephones were now a commercial reality, optical networking was becoming the norm for high-speed transport, and the strange domain known as the Internet was beginning to show its face to a curious public. The ongoing deregulation of the industry was creating interprovincial competition for the incumbent companies from such players as Rogers Communications and Primus Canada, in addition to Bell. Technology entrants were creating intermodal competition between fixed and wireless technologies. The new company created under Brian Canfield's leadership not only had to be good, it had to be quick. Otherwise it would be dead.

To Brian, "good" meant much more than technological proficiency. It meant offering nationwide service and diversifying into areas not yet offered by the company. He had an unwavering vision: "My primary reason for wanting to create a national carrier," he says, "was simple: scale and scope. The market down in the States served as a good example to draw lessons from. Consider this: Because of its massive geography, AT&T could go into a market and spread its operating costs across a huge pool of customers. We, on the other hand, were limited to amortizing our costs across a much smaller population base. The economics just didn't work. Furthermore, Bell was beginning to push into our territory, which represented another competitive force to be reckoned with. So we left Stentor and were very successful, and that gave us a thirst to say, 'We can do this better.' So we did."

Those were heady times for people in the company, but unnerving as well. In those days, TELUS Alberta and BC Tel were much like any other telephone company in North America. Employees started work at 7:30 AM; left shortly thereafter for their fifteen-minute coffee break, which often turned into a half-hour; took their half-hour lunch, which became an hour; did the same thing for breaks in the afternoon; and then left for home at 3:30 PM. There was little in the way of urgency; a prevailing sense of complacency came from the company's monopoly roots.

"When Bell announced that they were going national," recalls Josh Blair, "people were worried. When the two-province merger was announced between BC Tel and TELUS, one portion of the employee pool remained in the worry zone, while another portion, mostly the younger employees, people who had more of a competitive edge or were ready to embrace change, got excited about the prospect of this new stage in the company's trajectory. Brian painted a future where we had two choices. One was to sell out and let Bell Canada run everything from Montreal. Or we could remain a proud, strong company and have a future that included being nationally competitive. It was less about satiating people's fears and more about painting a picture of the future that showed a sincere upside. As a result, we saw renewed excitement among the employees. People wanted to be part of the future that Brian was painting, and as a result, a lot of that legacy behaviour got left behind where it belonged—in the past."

Blair remembers Brian Canfield's approach to melding the cultures of the two companies: "When we merged, half of the executive team had to be from Alberta, while the other half had to be from BC. That cascaded down several levels. And while it was the right thing to do from a tax perspective, it was extremely difficult to accomplish culturally. The two cultures were very different, and as a result, after the requisite period, the leaders from Alberta managed to move the BC people out of their organizations. The people from BC did the same, resulting in cultural silos within the company that Brian, once he found out about them, was not

going to allow. At one point, a member of the senior leadership team from the Alberta side issued an ultimatum, saying, 'If you're not going to let me run my part of the company the way I want to run it, I'm out of here.' So Brian said, 'Okay, then, take off.' Brian put into place a culture that said, 'I don't care where you're from. If you're the right person for the job, then you get the job—period.' Rather than try to promote from within and stick with a broken formula, he changed things around. The decision to *not* go with Bell was an outside-of-the-norm, gutsy decision, and rather than do what we'd always done, we changed the rules. And look where it got us."

The decision to merge the two companies was a bold, far-sighted move. Under Brian Canfield's leadership, TELUS was poised for the next step: to become a multimodal company that would expand beyond its traditional telephone-services roots. A new market beckoned, and Brian Canfield intended to be part of it.

CHAPTER 5

A FOCUS ON PEOPLE

BRIAN CANFIELD'S drive to succeed, his commitment to excellence, and his keen interest in technology weren't the only things that made him an effective executive. Arguably, his skill in managing his company's human resources had an even greater impact. The model he put in place for organizational transparency is still the hallmark of TELUS's uniqueness as a public company.

Historians of technology often claim that if we were tasked today with the responsibility of building a global telecommunications network, we would be hard-pressed to do so. The scope and complexity of that network, referred to by some as the largest, most complicated machine ever built by humankind, are beyond daunting. During the period this global network was being constructed, the telephone companies of the world were enormous too, with hundreds of thousands of people involved in the build-out. Today's companies are a fraction of that size.

Personnel development played a central role in the ability of the telephone industry to accomplish what it did. From the early days of telephones until well into the 1990s, the typical career path for most company employees was similar to the

FACING:
Brian initiated what came to be known as infonet sessions, in which he would conduct open forums to give employees throughout the company the opportunity to pose uncensored questions to senior executives. The practice was wildly successful and was part of the corporate commitment to open governance.

71

path Brian took: start at the bottom in a technology-centric craft position, usually doing physical labour as a union-represented employee; work hard to learn as much about the complex and varied technologies as possible; then, with luck, personal drive, and inclination, be promoted into an entry-level management position; and from there, over the course of many years, work your way up the management hierarchy to take on increasing levels of responsibility.

As a result of this standardized progression, most employees who found themselves in leadership positions were comfortable with technology, understood its central role in the delivery of services, and were able to engage with the people who worked for them on topics relevant to their increasingly technology-driven jobs.

Today, a growing number of management employees in telecommunications come into the ranks directly from university or from management positions in other industries. They are well educated and technologically adept, but they often lack a deep understanding of the application of technology in the service-provider realm and the culture of service that surrounds it. This kind of understanding comes only with time—it really can't be taught—and it is another dimension of the leadership formula that contributed greatly to Brian Canfield's success. Brian himself is quick to point out that many of his achievements were rooted in experience, beginning with his job as an apprentice equipment installer in 1956. "Every position I ever held gave me something," he says.

Lessons Learned

One of the most important lessons Brian learned during his progression from skilled craftsman to executive leader, he says, was that the best thing you can do is reward people on the basis of the work they do. "If you reward them for quality and commitment and for being a responsible member of the team," he says, "then people feel motivated to give their all to the effort at hand. I suppose that's what a meritocracy is all about. When I was in Engineering, I once received a letter from a supervisor telling me that I shouldn't be taking work home because it set a bad precedent. But you see, I had set a personal goal to get the job done correctly by a certain time, and if that meant taking work home, then I took it home. No one was going to dictate to me what I had to do to get the job that I was responsible for done, especially if it meant missing a commitment. I just don't work that way."

His commitment to both the job and to the customer also set Brian apart. "Back when I was an area general manager," he recalls, "we had a high-profile customer who called in with a serious problem: the people in his office were able to make outgoing calls from their offices, but they

couldn't receive any. Because I had worked in that part of the business not long before, I knew exactly what was wrong, and I also knew that it would get fixed. But it didn't, and the customer escalated the trouble to me. So I went down to the test desk and asked if anybody remembered that particular trouble ticket, and a guy said that he did and that he had put the ticket on the counter to be worked. I went over, found the ticket still sitting there, in spite of the fact that it was an escalated trouble, and said, 'Don't you know what the problem is? You should know this!' I headed down to the equipment bay with the technician following, trying to keep up. 'You have a blown fuse,' I told him, 'and the telltale [the indicator] hasn't popped all the way out to indicate a failure.' So I found the bad fuse, pulled it out, replaced it with a good one, and fixed the problem.

"As I said, I was the area general manager at the time, so it wasn't long before I got a call from the director. 'So, Brian,' he implored, 'is there any chance that you'd quit doing that?' I said, 'Here's the deal I'll make: I'll never go in there and fix equipment on my own again as long as someone else is there ready to do it. I promise that if it doesn't come to my attention, I won't get involved. I don't want to see customer trouble tickets sitting on a shelf with technicians standing around who could be working them.' "

Toward a Leadership Paradigm

Good leadership is often described as being difficult, complicated, and rare. In fact, good leadership is breathtakingly simple. Plainly put, it's an exercise in vision: good leaders help the people around them see what *could* be, not simply what is. Brian Canfield inspired the people around him at all levels to step up, to perform at higher levels, to challenge the status quo at every turn. Brian envisioned better ways to deliver customer service, and then demonstrated them through his personal bias for action—often to the consternation of those who worked for him. His thinking on the subject went beyond issues related to getting the job done or to the creation of a culture of service excellence. He also spent time thinking about the external focus that guided BC Tel and the industry in which it operated.

As telecommunications evolved and the industry became increasingly competitive, Brian realized that a structure was emerging from two components: the technology that made it possible to deliver products and services, and the regulatory decrees that tempered the manner in which companies did so. He saw technology as the motivator. Regulation was a necessary part of the service-delivery equation, he knew, but it often struggled to keep up with the feverish pace of technological change. Brian saw technology as an unstoppable force, a force that moved toward the future as it tried to keep up with the evolving demands of the marketplace. It was a force that the company he led must embrace if it was going to stay competitive and relevant. Brian believed that, to a certain extent, his industry was stochastic—meaning that it was governed by random and unpredictable events. Even when the events weren't random, their long-term impact often was. As a consequence, he worked hard

Brian A. Canfield
Mountainous Adventure

April 15, 1993
Chairman & CEO

October 1, 1990 President & CEO

November 1, 1972
TSPS Facilities Administrator

September 1, 1989
President & Chief
Operating Officer

September 1, 1971
Toll Traffic Network Supervisor

October 27, 1975
Consulting Analyst Management
Information Systems

January 1, 1988
Executive V.P.
Telephone Operations

March 1, 1968 Plant Assistant

March 14, 1966
Technician Engineering

June 1, 1976
DAISY Facilities
Supervisor

October 1, 1985
V.P. Technical Support

March 18, 1963
Central Office
Maintenance Man
Plant BC TEL

June 1, 1977
Facilities Coordinator
Operator Services

January 1, 1983
Area General
Manager Burnaby

July 1, 1960
Equipment Installer
CT&S

August 1, 1978
Material Manager
ST&B

June 26, 1981
Business Sales
Manager

June 28, 1956
Apprentice
Equipment
Installer CT&S

to build a corporate culture that was driven by excellence but was at the same time capable of flexibility.

Over the course of Brian's career, the company he worked for evolved from being a monopoly to one operating in a fully competitive environment. "During that time," he remembers, "whenever we had conversations about planning for the future, I used to say to the people I worked with, 'So, five years ago, would you have imagined that we'd be where we are today?' And they'd say no. I'd respond, 'So what makes you think you've got the next five years right?'

"The truth is that I knew where I'd been; I wanted to know where I was going. In those days, when you made a presentation to the board, you had all of these Mylar transparencies that you used with an overhead projector. I had this guy working for me who was an artist, and I had him draw a picture of me being picked up by balloons high enough that I could look over the next three hills. I inserted that drawing into my stack of transparencies whenever we had a meeting. I'd tell the board that that's the easy part—figuring out what's over those hills. The hard part is to get back to Earth, come back to today and figure out what it takes to win out there

An illustration created by TELUS for Brian on the day of his retirement from BC Tel, illustrating his perspective on vision and leadership.

beyond those hills. And that, remember, was during a period when nobody in telecommunications felt that they had a problem. The question I kept asking myself early on was this: How do you make a shift here [in the present] that's going to help you over here [in the future]?"

Brian's son Bruce, who works for TELUS, watched his father mature as a leader. During conversations with his father about telecommunications, he was amazed at his dad's ability to project into the future, regardless of whether that projection was in the realm of technology, service, or business.

Bruce also recalls some of his father's far-reaching decisions. During the time Brian Canfield was CEO, Bruce was a cable splicer in British Columbia's Lower Mainland. He worked on complex projects that included the design and installation of such technologically challenging programs as large-scale fibre builds. Bruce and his father would often talk about technology, but the conversation usually turned away from the technology itself, toward the topic of

engineering economics, a subject of great interest to Brian. Engineering economics is the process of solving technical problems while taking into account the economic viability of various options. One of the topics the two discussed frequently was the fact that work groups occasionally lose focus on strategic outcomes because they have a budget they are expected to meet or beat; that requirement shifts the focus to the tactical short term. One day, Brian decided he and Bruce should take an engineering economics course together at BCIT. The material turned out to be so valuable that Brian asked Josh Blair to make the course a requirement for all TELUS employees who were in engineering roles with responsibility for inside and outside plant as well as for transport. He wanted to make sure that people were looking at the big picture, not just at their own little part of the world.

Managing Change

One of Brian's earliest observations as a leader was that there was a great deal of self-importance and level consciousness in his organization, which he felt detracted from otherwise positive activities. "It really bothered me that there were rules around who you could and couldn't talk to," he says. "That always seemed counterproductive to me. Even the steps required to move from job title to job title were silly. Either a person was qualified and deserved the position, or they weren't. And those who weren't were pretty obvious.

"Another thing I wasn't able to tolerate," continues Brian, "was people who either refused to or were incapable of thinking innovatively. I'll give you a classic example. Before computers became common we had [paper] forms for everything. If somebody came up with a new requirement or procedure for something, even if it replaced something else and made the original thing obsolete, they'd just add another page to the package of forms. But nobody ever took anything out! It reminds me of security regulations that just keep getting fatter and fatter, until you have a book that no one can read, and as a result, security doesn't get done the way it should. If

you had the temerity to actually try something different, to slim down that packet of forms, you were seen as something of a troublemaker."

Brian reflects on his own career as a troublemaker with amusement. "I did a lot of that. I had guys who always had huge sheets of brown paper on the walls covered with system flowcharts, because I'd say to them, 'Flowchart for me what *should* happen, not the way it works today.' I even had a thing I put together while I was CEO called Getting Rid of Dumb Rules (some remember it as the War on Waste). I invited the guy who was the head of Human Resources at the time to get a group of people together who wouldn't be intimidated by being in a meeting with the CEO. I tend to get into things pretty loudly sometimes, and I don't mean to intimidate people, but I needed people who could see past that—that was the main criterion. And I told the HR executive that I wanted them from all different walks, from all different parts of the company, and from all levels. I got them into a room and I said, 'We all know from working out there—they were all managers—that there are things we do that waste time and resources.' I challenged and empowered them to embrace the notion of questioning everything we did in their individual organizations, to ferret out things we did that were dumb. It was so successful that GTE recognized the power of this innovative process and took the entire team down to Connecticut for a formal recognition event to celebrate what we had accomplished.

"Bottom line? I don't like self-important people. A person should be recognized for what they deserve; you shouldn't have to tell anybody about it. And I realized that failure to keep up with change is the kiss of death. Monopolies have never been really big on innovation because, honestly, there's no need for it. After all, where else are customers going to go?"

Change or Die

Brian is quick to heap praise on those who came before him. "Gordon MacFarlane was the antithesis of fossilized behaviour," he says. "He's very, very innovative, even today.

What made him so successful was that he was always looking for ways to innovate in the business. I learned a lot from him. The truth is that there's always a bit of a gap between the CEO and the people who are trying to get things done, and it tends to be counterproductive. I was always looking for ways to narrow that gap."

MacFarlane, who preceded Brian Canfield as chief executive at BC Tel, was an exceptional leader who led the transformation of BC Tel into one of the most desirable workplaces in Canada, and set the stage for the creation of TELUS.

During his career he was recognized repeatedly for his contributions to the country. In 1988 he received the life achievement award from the federal Department of Communications for his role in developing communication technology, and in 1991 was inducted into the Order of British Columbia.

Today, Gordon MacFarlane lives the good life. He's in his early 90s and a bit hard of hearing, but neither of those have slowed him down: he

and his wife routinely travel North America in a 37-foot motor home. He remembers his time with Brian Canfield with affection.

From the first time I had contact with Brian, I was impressed that he always performed at a level well beyond that of his peers, and perhaps more importantly, beyond my own expectations— no matter how demanding they were. After seeing this time and time again, I realized that Brian wasn't simply doing what he was asked to do; he was doing what he loved to do—to overcome challenges.

In fact, it didn't take me long to realize that if he wasn't presented with a challenge, he'd invent one. For example, he would learn a new word every evening after work, frequently Latin, and the next day he would find the perfect occasion to use it. That afforded him two challenges—first, to learn the word, and second, to engineer an opportunity to put it to use.

I also realized that the sum of the challenges he was being presented with, together with those he created, were well beyond the ability of a single person to manage. Brian solved this particular challenge by perfecting his inborn skills at motivating others to enroll in the resolution of any given challenge. He became so good at it that in addition to motivating his entire work force, he managed to convince me to serve as his volunteer worker, cleaning ditches—and loving it!

Given these skills, it's no wonder that Brian had such a uniquely successful career, serving both his industry and his country. Brian has always been an inspiration to me, and I feel fortunate and proud to know him.

Brian's efforts with regard to "narrowing the gap" are legendary in the company. One of the first areas he went after was employee communication: keeping the troops informed. "One thing my dad always recognized as being very important," says Bruce Canfield, "is the need to keep the employees informed. Clearly, there are some things you can't talk about, but as it relates to the company, the strategy, where we're headed, he always had a desire, starting when he was an area general manager, to let people know what was going on. He created these things called infonet sessions, using video and audio conferencing across British Columbia, long before it was a common corporate practice. He would send members of his senior team out to the larger centres so there would be an executive presence there during the sessions. He would originate them from the Boot [the TELUS building in Burnaby, British Columbia, so-called because of its distinctive shape and now renamed the Brian Canfield Centre for Excellence in Telecommunications].

"One of the things we have at the building is a large auditorium that seats about 180 people. It's perfect for meetings, and it was perfect for the infonet sessions that my dad conducted. The idea was that any employee, regardless of position, rank, or level, could ask him any question they liked. As long as he could answer it without violating a necessary confidentiality, he'd answer it. I remember being in the audience during one of those sessions when a union member came up and tried to corner him into an argument about jobs being lost as the result of the implementation of new technology. I cringed, because there's one thing I know about my dad: he's a straight shooter. Don't ask the question if you don't want to hear the answer. He was professional about it, he wasn't rude, but he gave it to her with both barrels and backed up everything he said with verifiable fact. Everyone

respected him because he held nothing back and went straight to the point. Some people don't know what they're in for when they start that kind of thing.

"Here's another example. In any building, sooner or later, the elevators break down. One time at the Boot the elevator broke down for an extended period of time while my dad was heading back to his office. So he said to everyone on the elevator, 'Well, you have a unique opportunity. Here we are, not sure how long we'll be together, so does anybody have any questions they want to ask me?' That's just the way he is: approachable. That was why everybody liked him."

It was through these actions and others like them that Brian worked to knock down the barriers between the top leaders in the company and the team members who wanted more insight from those leaders. The transparency culture he established at BC Tel continues at TELUS to this day.

Throughout his career, Brian Canfield subscribed to a philosophy of deliberate, intelligently executed change and the imperative to embrace it as a way forward. In their book *Blown to Bits: How the New Economics of Information Transforms Strategy,* authors Philip Evans and Thomas S. Wurster make an observation about successful leaders that could easily be about Brian:

> A greater vulnerability than legacy assets is a legacy mindset. It may be easy to grasp this point intellectually, but it is profoundly difficult in practice. Managers must put aside the presuppositions of the old competitive world and compete according to totally new rules of engagement. They must make decisions at a different speed, long before the numbers are in place and the plans formalized. They must acquire totally new technical and entrepreneurial skills, quite different from what made their organization (and them personally) so successful. They must manage for maximal opportunity, not minimum risk. They must devolve decision making, install different reward structures and perhaps even devise different ownership structures. They have little choice. If they don't do it for their own business, somebody else will do it to them.

Eliminating legacy mindsets, adopting new technologies, taking decisive action before the facts are all in hand, and managing for maximum opportunity, rather than minimum risk, were hallmark characteristics of Brian Canfield's leadership. And fortuitously so. By 1998, the Canadian telecom industry was in the throes of violent reinvention. Change was in the wind, but it was shaping up to be more like a Category 5 hurricane, and Brian was in its eye. A national company was about to be born, and it would change Canada—and the industry—forever.

CHAPTER 6

PIVOTAL MOMENTS

THE YEAR WAS 1999, and Brian Canfield was at a crossroads.

Around the world, the telecommunications industry was in tectonic upheaval. Rarely in the history of modern business had an industry gone through such wrenching change, seen so many emergent opportunities, encountered so many diverse competitive threats, or had so much investment money thrown its direction in so short a time. Telecom, once a largely invisible sector to all but those who worked in it, had become a hot commodity: everyone wanted a piece of the action. But it wasn't just about telecom anymore, and Brian saw the writing on the proverbial wall. A new phenomenon had emerged that was changing the face of the technology sector, and telecom was squarely in its sights. This phenomenon, known as convergence, would guide a series of decisions that Brian knew he had to make to thrust his company onto the national—and, ultimately, international—stage.

Historically, the telephone industry—and to a lesser degree, telecom—had always been a vertically integrated, hierarchically structured, single-function business. Voice was the name of the game, and long distance was the cash cow. Information

FACING:
Brian Canfield responds to a question during a talk delivered to a BC Tel audience.

technology, better known by its acronym IT, was a necessary annoyance at first, tolerated as a significant cost item that offered dubious value—and clearly didn't offer anywhere near the potential for riches that telecom brought to the table.

But that was changing, and quickly. Voice was no longer in the pole position, and thanks to alternative transport schemes driven largely by the growing proliferation of IP (Internet protocol), long-distance revenue was in free fall. IT was emerging as a growing revenue opportunity. IP, the underlying operating protocol for the Internet, was now seen as the future of the industry—a driving force that was compelling telephone companies to reconsider their commitment to legacy circuit switching, the mainstay of their industry, and to think seriously about the steps required to migrate to an all-IP infrastructure. That's what convergence was all about: the collapsing of multiple technologies into a single transport fabric.

Convergence wasn't limited to technology. In the years leading up to the collapse of the telecom bubble in 2001, company convergence was the name of the game, with a mergers-and-acquisitions feeding frenzy underway. Cisco, a major player in the Internet hardware game, acquired dozens of corporations and became the most valuable company in the world with a market cap of well over $500 billion. Nortel Networks, Lucent Technologies, and a host of others gobbled up smaller companies, growing wildly as their share prices climbed. Internet service provider AOL acquired media giant Time Warner in a transaction that at the time was seen as prescient but after the fact as an object lesson in hubris and poor planning. Most important of all, though, was the growth of services convergence. Companies began to heed the market's siren song: "It's not about the technology… it's about the services."

Brian Canfield followed these developments with fierce intensity.

He realized that he was witness to the birth of a new industry, one that would have a profound impact on every business on the planet. Technology, services, and company convergence were happening across the global technology industry. Telephony remained an important service to customers, but data and all that it represented would soon outpace, outperform, and out-earn voice. The evolution to an all-IP network was a *when* question, not an *if* question, for TELUS. His company would also have to reformulate its definition of service if it intended to be a long-term, relevant player.

Brian had been named chairman of the company when BC Tel and TELUS Alberta merged in 1999. He explains the sequence of events that defined the period: "I retired as the CEO of BC Tel in July 1997 because it was time, and I became the non-executive chairman of the firm. At that time, Stentor was still alive and strong, but I knew that a new structure was needed. We had to do something to retain our competitive position.

FACING:
In this photograph, outdoor plant technicians install a large copper cable under the streets of Vancouver. Today, a single optical fibre with the diameter of a human hair transports tens of thousands of times the bandwidth of this entire copper cable.

"This was something of a difficult time for us managerially. Don Calder, the gentleman who had followed me and was CEO for eighteen months, had moved on, and George Petty had been brought in from AT&T in the States via Alberta to run the company. We were looking to acquire Clearnet, and George wanted to do a cash purchase. But at the time we really couldn't afford that kind of a cash outlay. As chairman, I kept telling George that we had to get our stock price up and then use that as currency for the deal, but he was opposed to that strategy. Ultimately, he wanted to put it to a vote at the board, but I knew that he'd be turned down. To save any embarrassment, I asked for a straw vote before the meeting. I went around the table and asked, 'If we were to put this [plan for a cash purchase] to a vote, how would you vote for it?' I went around the whole table, and there was only one supporter."

Petty realized his plan would not pass, and ultimately he left his position as chief executive. This left the company without a CEO, and the board asked Brian if he would be willing to step back into the job temporarily. He told them he had promised his wife he wouldn't be travelling as much, so he would need to discuss the offer with her first. She understood that it was important, so she consented. "But she also suggested," says Brian, "that I ask to be given a place to live in in Victoria as part of my compensation. At that point, she pulled out a brochure and showed it to me—she'd obviously already been thinking about this. I told her that we'd better just buy a place, so we did. I think I'm the only person in history who ever had to spend hundreds of thousands of dollars to go back to work."

The next day, the board held a meeting to formalize Brian's acceptance of the role of CEO. He stepped into the position in September 1999, but he made it clear that his willingness was contingent on an active search for a person to replace him.

The decision to merge TELUS Alberta and BC Tel under Brian's leadership had been a bold, far-sighted move. The larger, more capable TELUS offered local and long-distance

service in the country's western-most provinces. But that was still a far cry from being national. If TELUS was going to offer service across Canada, it needed a wireline and wireless presence across all the provinces and territories.

Geographic Expansion

Back in the CEO role on an interim basis, Brian Canfield found his gaze turning toward Quebec. The province had important technology centres, including Montreal, Quebec City, and Rimouski, and a wealth of highly trained human capital. Quebec was home to a young and sophisticated user base, and an increasingly diverse technology sector.

The Corporation de Téléphone et de Pouvoir de Québec, founded in 1927, became Québec-Téléphone in 1955. In 1966, the GTE subsidiary Anglo-Canadian became a majority shareholder. GTE held a similar position within BC Tel. When BC Tel and TELUS Alberta merged, GTE sold its ownership position in Québec-Téléphone to TELUS. On March 31,

2000, TELUS agreed to acquire 70 per cent of QuébecTel Group: 49 per cent of the company from public minority shareholders and 21 per cent from GTE. Québec-Téléphone became TELUS Québec on April 2, 2001, the transaction completed on August 15, 2001.

The acquisition offered advantages to all of the involved parties. TELUS became a nationwide provider of telecommunications services, but not just that. Avoiding the cost of a capital-intensive infrastructure build-out in the province saved not only a substantial capital outlay but also an equally valuable commodity: time. Lost-opportunity cost in the world of technology can be fatal. The acquisition of QuébecTel saved TELUS at least two years of cost without having to endure the loss of parallel revenue.

Brian Canfield had this to say on the day the agreement was signed:

> TELUS is committed to its national strategy. For TELUS, this accelerates its entry into Quebec by almost two years and provides a strong management

team with deep market knowledge, together with an experienced employee base. It's a truly remarkable, strategic fit. QuébecTel will play a significant role in leading the execution of the TELUS strategy in Quebec, and we expect that a meaningful part of the execution of this strategy will be managed and staffed from the current head office in Rimouski.

Because of the pre-existing ownership structure shared with BC Tel, GTE retained a 20.5 per cent ownership position in TELUS after the QuébecTel acquisition. When GTE merged with Bell Atlantic in 2000 to form Verizon, Verizon became the holder of that ownership position, until divesting its holdings in 2004.

Brian Canfield's role was evolving as well. In July 2000, he became chairman of the corporation, ceding the role of CEO to Darren Entwistle. One of their first strategic moves together was the Clearnet acquisition, which resulted in TELUS's wireless service expanding from British Columbia and Alberta to become national. Similar to the QuébecTel acquisition, acquiring Clearnet's infrastructure, human capital, and customer base bought TELUS time. Had the company been forced to build a wireless network east of Alberta from scratch, the effort would have taken at least three years and have cost significantly more. In a market as ferociously competitive as Canada's wireless environment, with such players as Bell Mobility and Rogers Communications chomping at the bit, three years was an eternity—and quite possibly a deal breaker. The Clearnet acquisition was a game changer for TELUS, and it marked the beginning of what proved to be an effective partnership between two great leaders.

Changing of the Guard

The transition from one CEO to another can be fraught with danger because of the potential for disruption. Micheline Bouchard, a member of the TELUS board, watched with admiration as Brian Canfield

The board's decision to hire Darren as the replacement CEO for Brian was a reflection of the company's—and Brian's—commitment to a new era of service, and the requirement of a new executive perspective to make it happen.

executed a series of what were construed by many as contrarian moves. "That says a lot about an individual," she muses. "When we exited the former CEO following the BC Tel-TELUS Alberta merger, Brian came back as the interim CEO. A lot of people might have seen that as a way for him to parachute back in to be the hero and the leader of national expansion. But that's not what he did. Instead he said, 'This isn't me. We need a different person at the helm with different thinking, a different vision, a different runway, a different place in his or her career to make this national expansion happen.' It had to be tempting to step in and be that hero, but instead he said, 'I don't have the skills to do it

at the level where we need it to be.' So we went out and found Darren."

Brian understood well what TELUS needed to do to maintain its forward momentum, and he knew he wasn't the person to lead that next step. "Brian set the stage for our national expansion as a company," Bouchard explains. "He didn't have the plan or the ingredients to make it successful, but he created the vision we needed to carve it out for ourselves. You know the expression that if you have a really talented individual, you hand them a challenge that most believe isn't really solvable? That's what Brian did—he handed the challenge of national expansion to Darren and then gave him the space to make it happen. Brian then stepped into the role of governance, leaving the role of management and, ultimately, organizational leadership, to Darren.

"Brian also had the benefit of understanding and liking technology, as does Darren. That was important at the time, because the technology was changing and evolving at a blinding pace, and we couldn't risk falling behind. The truth is that they're both visionaries, and they worked exceptionally well together."

Mel Cooper also remembers the period well. "I was one of three people to be appointed to the search committee that was tasked with finding the new CEO," he says. "Those were exciting times, but it was bittersweet, because we knew that we were replacing Brian Canfield. We had a national search company working for us, and they went about looking for candidates. We were searching the world—people from Singapore, the States, and Canada showed up on the shortlist of potential executives. And while they were all very good, I had some concerns about them that came from my history with the company.

"When we created TELUS, we all knew there was a strong difference of cultures between Alberta and British Columbia that we had to manage carefully if we were to get the best of both and make them part of the new merged enterprise. That was very important, and that thinking was going on in my head while we were looking at those potential CEOs. When we finally had a list of people

Mel Cooper, former TELUS and BC Tel board member, and current Chair of the TELUS Victoria Community Board.

we were determined to interview, we invited each of them to Vancouver for a first meeting.

"Their bios were less important than their ability to think strategically and to respond to what at the time was the fastest-changing industry in the country, perhaps in the world. When we looked over the top four or so, I had my doubts about them because they all looked like old telephone-company people—they had all come out of the telephone business that in many ways we were leaving behind. TELUS had already introduced mobility, and would soon add TV, Internet and other services. We embraced those new capabilities long before others did, which is why I was concerned that an executive from the legacy telephone industry might not have the vision to see beyond what they knew. We realized as well that the Internet needed to be a big part of our future, and leadership had to understand that as well."

While the TELUS search committee was considering the shortlist of candidates, its executive search firm in Toronto called to ask if it would be willing to add one more person to the list. The headhunter explained that this additional candidate was very different from the others. "This is a guy who you might not initially consider, but I think you should look at him seriously," he told the search committee.

Darren Entwistle was a fast-rising executive in Europe, working for Cable & Wireless Communications. One afternoon, Darren and his CEO were on their way to a meeting when the CEO's phone rang. It was a member of the executive search team, calling the CEO to seek his opinion about one of the candidates they were considering. After his boss hung up, Darren, curious, asked what the call had been about. The CEO explained it was a call from a search company looking for a CEO for a "small regional telephone company in Canada." When Darren, who is Canadian, got home that night, he chatted with his wife, telling her, "We may have a chance to get back to Canada—I want to pursue that." She agreed, and the next day Darren contacted the search firm and tossed his name into the hat.

The TELUS search committee arranged for Darren to travel to Vancouver. Committee members met with him for several hours, then asked him to step out for a few minutes so they could have a private discussion about the meeting so far. As soon as Darren left the room, Mel Cooper remembers, one of the committee members said, "Did we just have a tornado go through this room, or was it a hurricane?" They had fired hypothetical questions at Darren about business strategy, economics, regulation, and a host of other topics. His responses were so complete and well-thought-out that he gave the impression he was delivering a prepared speech on each of the topics. Ultimately, the TELUS search committee told the board that even though Darren was young, he was impressively different from all the other candidates, and it strongly recommended him for the position.

Although Darren's age was a mild concern for the board members—he was just thirty-seven at the time—they quickly came to the realization that all top people in the modern information and communications technology industry (Michael Dell at Dell, Bill Gates at Microsoft, Jeff Bezos at Amazon, and Steve Jobs at Apple, to name a few) were all very young—and very successful. They offered him the position, and he accepted. He was appointed as the new CEO of TELUS in July 2000.

Darren Entwistle remembers his early days at TELUS as a time filled with equal parts excitement and dread. "We were still working through the process of aligning two very different cultures," he says, "something that Brian threw his heart and soul into. Somewhere along the way, Brian was informed that as soon as they found a new CEO—which turned out to be me—he could be the chairman of the board, but he would be a non-executive chair with no involvement in the business and no office in the building. This all happened before I arrived. You can imagine how disappointed Brian was. So when I came on board, I was already one of his least favourite people on the planet and he hadn't even met me yet.

"So there I was trying to drive the new strategy, and as you can imagine, my relationship with Brian was very tense—until a pivotal moment occurred, which was when we had a true heart-to-heart conversation. We got together one day, and I told him that I needed him involved in the business and that I absolutely wanted him to have an office in the building. I truly needed his advice and wisdom. I always called Brian the original 'chief commonsense officer' of TELUS. 'Your perspective,' I told him, 'is crucial to me. I need you to support the strategy as we make big bets on wireless and data, and as we go from a regional to a national focus. We're changing the leadership team, and we're changing the culture. We don't have one company; we have BC Tel, TELUS Alberta, QuébecTel and Clearnet, and we have to make this into a single, unified company behind a single, unified strategy, then animate that in the hearts and minds of the employees and shareholders.' We had that meeting just after I completed my first year, and that made all the difference. The truth is, what has given the company the ability to survive the various equity meltdowns and credit crunches we've experienced is that we've always had the right strategy, the right team, and we've executed well through every exogenous predicament we've encountered—and still delivered a total shareholder return of 335 per cent—68 percentage points ahead of the next closest competitor on the MSCI [Morgan Stanley Capital International] World Index. I credit Brian with the vision and hard work required to make that happen successfully. Without his guidance, it never would have happened."

From Brian's perspective, Darren took over the reins at TELUS at the perfect time for a leadership transition. "Darren came in July, and by August we had acquired Clearnet. We'd been working on that deal for months, trying to get GTE to see their way through the process. During my nine months in the position, I talked GTE into selling us QuébecTel, which gave us a presence in British Columbia, Alberta and Quebec, and then Darren added Clearnet. In the meantime, we had already started the build-out of our fibre rings. I got it started, but let's give due credit: Darren was the one who assembled all the pieces.

"Those were somewhat difficult times. We were bringing together all of those different companies, each of them with unique cultures and personalities and expectations. Some days it was like dealing with the feud between the Hatfields and the McCoys. It was fortuitous that Darren was—and is—such a strong leader and has such a strong personality. He's a truly Stentorian voice. And he's exceptionally clever. He has tremendous presence and an ability to just get things done. He was the perfect match for the position."

By 2000, Brian had been a valuable TELUS employee for more than four decades, and he had become a gifted leader. Now, as chairman of the board, he was moving into an important new role. He would position TELUS at the vanguard of organizational transparency, challenging the entire industry to follow suit. And even though he had retired as CEO, he hadn't stopped working. In his final years as the chief executive of TELUS, he positioned the company as the paragon of responsible corporate citizenship.

FACING:
Brian Canfield, the original "chief commonsense officer" at TELUS.

CHAPTER 7

BUILDING A MODEL OF TRANSPARENT GOVERNANCE

IT'S AN IRONY of the business world that corporate governance is most visible when it's missing. During the chaotic years of the telecom bubble, which in 2001 culminated in collapse, and the ensuing evaporation of roughly $7 trillion of tech-sector market value, the *lack* of governance was perhaps the most visible aspect of corporate behaviour. The companies that found themselves in the public spotlight weren't those that, through perseverance and good business practices, managed to survive the collapse, but rather those that had precipitated it—companies like Enron, WorldCom, Arthur Andersen, Global Crossing, and Nortel, to name a few.

Good governance practice is top of mind in most public companies today. But for Brian Canfield, good governance was more than a business practice. It was a personal philosophy, and he dedicated himself to it with characteristic ferocity. "Governance is key, and it was Brian's main thrust," says Micheline Bouchard, who's been a TELUS corporate board member since 2004. "Brian was always a strong advocate for shareholders' rights. He strongly believed in doing what was right for those he spoke for and represented."

99

*Micheline Bouchard,
TELUS board member
and friend of Brian.*

TELUS is a publicly traded corporation and as such is required to maintain a degree of separation between corporate ownership and corporate control. Owners expect a return on their investment, and that return is in no small part thanks to the decisions management makes on the corporation's behalf. A part of the contract shareholders make with the company is the delegation of managerial decisions to the board of directors, which in turn delegates responsibilities to the company's management team.

In order for the relationship between the chair of the corporation, the board of directors, and the shareholders to work, a governance model must be in place to align the roles, responsibilities, and incentives of all the groups involved in the day-to-day operation of the organization. The intent is straightforward: to protect shareholders and their investments, and to give managers and directors a realistic sense of accountability toward the shareholders. Good governance practices can include separating the roles and responsibilities of the CEO and the chair; ensuring that the board of directors has a majority of outside (non-employee) members; creating systems that guarantee full disclosure of such things as executive compensation and financial data; and imposing binding restrictions that limit the power of management, and prevent a dominant shareholder from taking control of the company through a hostile act.

When Brian Canfield became chairman of TELUS, he developed an abiding interest in governance practices. To his way of thinking, it was essential that the board acts as transparently as was prudent, not only with the public but also with each other. He engaged personally in the development of governance practices that still guide TELUS today, including a program through which company directors assess themselves and their peers. Several times a year, for example, Brian would schedule one-on-one meetings with each corporate director to go over business results and have an open conversation about how governance practices could be improved. He prepared

exhaustively for those meetings. "To act on the basis of your beliefs, and to seek results, was part of Brian's basic fabric as a human being," recalls Micheline Bouchard. "That's what he did in terms of corporate governance. Brian is all about being fair. He isn't shy about fighting for what he believes in. And yet he's a sensitive person who shares common interests with the people he stands for and defends. For Brian, the focus was always on results, not himself. That's what made him such an effective leader."

HR Governance

To Josh Blair, Brian Canfield was more than an effective leader; he was a mentor. Josh would go to Brian with thorny issues, many of them highly sensitive, and Brian would provide feedback that allowed Josh to come to the best solution. Never would Brian offer up an answer, Josh says; instead, he would listen, make a few insightful suggestions, and then allow Josh to answer the question himself.

As TELUS's chief corporate officer, and the person responsible for the

development and execution of the corporation's global human resources strategy, Josh Blair is wholly preoccupied with corporate governance—it lies at the heart of everything he does. He is also very involved in human resources governance, a critical corollary that is poorly understood in many companies.

Historically, HR organizations covered such things as salary management, retirement programs, and personnel and organizational structure. Many companies failed to address a far more important issue: governance that addresses leadership and management practices at the top, which in turn leads to improved organizational performance. HR governance guides strategic decisions related to company employees and the best use of human capital. If done correctly, HR governance leads to better prioritization of business decisions, improved financial acumen, cleaner delineation of job definitions, clearly articulated professional development paths for employees, and stronger, more focused executive decision making. HR governance isn't a corporate objective but, rather, an approach. Brian Canfield's belief in a merit-based approach to motivation and reward aligns perfectly with the goals of HR governance. And during his time as chairman, Brian put into place numerous structures at the board level that fundamentally changed the way TELUS assesses its own performance. Those structures remain in place today.

The first of these is a comprehensive risk management framework, in which the top one thousand leaders at TELUS are surveyed every year. They are asked a variety of questions about the key risks they believe face the company over the next few years. Their answers are synthesized, and every quarter, the executive team looks at the list to determine the top fifty risks the company could encounter. Each scenario is given both a relative risk rating and what TELUS refers to as a risk resiliency adjusted rating. The information this analysis yields is reviewed with the board of directors also every quarter. As a result, the board can devote its attention to risk identification and risk management in the medium to long term—the horizon the senior leadership

team of any organization should be focused on as well.

Brian Canfield intuitively understood the strategic alignment that must be nurtured between corporate governance practices and governance practices designed to maximize human potential. Business strategy comes first: it determines the long-term goals and direction of the organization. Once those goals are agreed to, though, strategies must be put in place from top to bottom to make the most of a skilled and productive team. A well-designed and properly executed HR strategy details how employees are hired, developed, motivated, and managed, in ways that support the goals and mission of the organization. While Darren Entwistle is widely known as a world-leading thought and practice leader in the realm of human capital development, Brian Canfield too was masterful at supporting this approach at the board level.

As chairman, he established a practice in which each corporate director rates the other directors. The results go to the chairman, who develops a relative performance ranking

FACING:
Josh Blair with Brian Canfield, presenting a cheque for $5,000 to British Columbia's Delta Hospice Society.

for all of the TELUS board members. Brian conducted performance discussions with each director on an annual basis, the goal of which was to celebrate their strengths, identify opportunities for improvement, let them know if they were seen as being too domineering or not adequately engaged on certain topics, and so on. This level of engagement is rarely seen at the board level, yet, since Brian's time, it has been a part of the leadership equation at TELUS. Lou Sekora was the mayor of Coquitlam when the city hosted the BC Summer Games and BC Seniors Games in 1991. "Brian," Sekora says, "was instrumental in bringing the BC Summer Games to Coquitlam and establishing the Coquitlam Foundation. He has powerful, long-range vision. But just as important, he's also a great motivator. He knew how to put a board together and get the most from every single member."

The Mason Capital Adventure

As chairman of the corporation, Brian was driven to do the right thing for TELUS, for the company's employees, and for the shareholders, even in the face of criticism. He understood better than most that *popular* doesn't mean *right*. He had a higher calling: to build a national service provider focused on the customer and on the reliable delivery of competitive and more innovative products and services. These beliefs served him well when an opportunistic investor with little interest in the well-being of the company or the value of the company's shares tried to exert control over TELUS.

During Brian's early years as chairman, TELUS had two classes of shares, initially created to comply with foreign-ownership restrictions when TELUS's shareholder base included significant foreign ownership. One class was voting shares that could be traded only in Canada; the other was non-voting shares traded in both Canada and the United States, on the Toronto and New York stock exchanges. The non-voting shares did not carry the right to vote in all circumstances, but they did have the same economic attributes as the voting shares, though still traded at a discount.

In 2012, with the level of foreign ownership decreased, the TELUS Board of Directors decided to eliminate the dual-class share structure to enhance the company's competitiveness through increased share liquidity and the adoption of best practices in corporate governance. The decision to convert the non-voting shares to voting shares on a one-for-one basis was a dicey move, as there was a risk that shareholders who owned voting shares might reject the plan. But Brian, Darren, and the rest of the board felt that it was the right thing to do for all concerned.

In February of that year, following the announcement of the proposed one-for-one share conversion, the gap between the non-voting and voting shares significantly narrowed. In April, a New York-based hedge fund, Mason Capital, announced that it had acquired nearly 20 per cent of TELUS's voting stock, valued at almost $2 billion, and that it intended to oppose the proposal. To finance these holdings, Mason basically sold short the non-voting shares it had borrowed and used the proceeds to acquire a roughly equivalent number of voting shares. Mason was gambling that the TELUS proposal would be voted down by shareholders, and that the spread between the value of the non-voting shares and the voting shares would reappear, allowing the firm to realize a substantial short-term return.

By taking this position, however, Mason telegraphed to the world that it had little interest in the future of TELUS—whether the common stock went up or down, it didn't really care. Mason was throwing its considerable weight around for the sole purpose of generating a short-term profit on the price spread of TELUS shares. In addition, because Mason's long common share position roughly equalled its short non-voting position, it controlled nearly 20 per cent of the vote yet held a nominal net economic interest in TELUS. This practice is known as "empty voting" and is frowned upon in most markets, particularly when it places a swath of shareholders at an economic disadvantage. As chairman of TELUS, Brian Canfield had to help determine the right path for the company.

"Longevity in the company and in the industry gave Brian the ability to see both the good and the bad in terms of corporate governance," says Darren Entwistle, "and this was as true with regard to the Mason situation as any other challenge he faced as a TELUS leader. Brian's definition of good governance was driven by his own set of professional values, not by what some consultant or the self-serving leaders of a hedge fund think good governance should be. His view on the subject came from being a business operator. His view of governance came from his personal integrity, his sense of righteousness, his belief in transparency and honesty, and his sense of duty and responsibility to do right by multiple stakeholder constituencies—not just shareholders, but all securities stakeholders, on both the equity and the debt sides of the equation.

"He also thought about governance in terms of employees and communities," says Entwistle. "That's what we call 'fair process.' It's how we tackle our challenges, engage our team members, explore options for answering those challenges, decide what's best to do, and then explain why a particular option is selected. It's all about executing the option we chose and then evaluating it from an organizational learning and development perspective. And that's what guided Brian and the board during this difficult time."

Mason Capital pulled out all the stops in its battle to win against the TELUS board. Initially, the firm argued that TELUS's actions would hand over "free money" to non-voting shareholders, thus diluting the position held by voting shareholders. It also argued that TELUS's directors were operating under a conflict of interest, since 89 per cent of their total holdings were in non-voting shares. TELUS countered with the arguments that the loss of the discount would be more than made up for in additional liquidity, and that the discount would become irrelevant in the fullness of time, as the company's articles expressly planned for a one-for-one share conversion upon foreign-ownership regulations being sunset by the federal government (an outcome that is generally accepted as a foregone conclusion).

In the interest of all shareholders, TELUS withdrew its conversion plan in May but reiterated its desire to secure the benefits of a simplified structure at some point in the future. Mason saw it as a win, but the war was far from over. TELUS's statement of intent caught the market's attention, which caused the non-voting and voting share price spread to remain in place—ironically locking Mason into its investment and depriving it of its expected profit.

The game recommenced with a new TELUS proposal in August, and in reaction, Mason called for a special shareholder meeting to force a vote that would amend TELUS's articles. Effectively, its plan was to eliminate the board's ability to convert the non-voting shares without a discount. Mason called for the meeting to be held in Burnaby at 10 AM on October 17—the same day the TELUS special shareholder meeting to consider the revised proposal was scheduled to take place, also in Burnaby, four hours later.

Checkmate

The battle played out in front of shareholders and the courts, with TELUS's proposal coming out overwhelmingly victorious. Mason Capital's arbitrage strategy and motivation raised concerns among shareholders such that Mason's attempt to convince shareholders that its actions were in their best interest proved futile. Between February and August 2012, TELUS's total market value had grown by $2 billion. Had Mason simply taken a long position on TELUS shares, it would have been far better off. As it was, Mason found itself locked in with no place to go.

Brian Canfield's position on behalf of the board wasn't so much about thwarting the efforts of a specific shareholder seeking to exercise undue influence as it was about protecting TELUS's broader base of long-standing shareholders—and TELUS itself. Although some of the best-performing corporations in Canada have a dual-class share structure, the model was facing growing opposition, largely led by institutional investors. The Canadian Coalition for Good Governance, an organization formed by twenty-three of Canada's leading institutional investors, also opposes dual-class share structures, on the grounds that they don't lead to good overall corporate citizenship. Another reason for moving to a single class of shares also drove Brian, Darren, and the TELUS board: studies indicate that companies with single-class share structures tend to outperform those with dual-class. The position taken by the TELUS board was corporate governance at its best.

From TELUS to the World

Mel Cooper, a former board member of both BC Tel and TELUS, has, like Brian, been a major supporter of community initiatives throughout his long and distinguished career. He and Brian became close during the years they worked together on the board, and he remembers their time together fondly. "Brian was always ahead of the game with regard to board policies and practices," Mel says. "Early on, I found Brian to be very precise and professional, a leading-edge CEO. For many years, I was a member of the Governance Committee, and Brian was committed to having the best-run governance program of any company in British Columbia and eventually

in Canada." TELUS became a leader in this regard. At one point, in fact, Cooper was forced to leave the board because a strategic decision set the age limit for membership at sixty-five and, at age seventy, he was in violation of that. Cooper chuckles about it. "I was chairman of the committee that came up with that decision, so I effectively caused my own demise!"

"Once Brian was happy with governance at TELUS," continues Cooper, "he started to get involved nationally." According to Cooper, during the late 1990s, many companies were committing fully to the right kinds of governance. "Brian was a leader there," Cooper says, "because in his mind there was never a doubt that it was the right thing to do."

Brian made an effort to share TELUS's beliefs and practice as widely as he could, ultimately joining the Canadian Public Accountability Board. During his years as TELUS chairman, he also served on the boards of some of Canada's best-known companies, including Terasen, Suncor Energy, Royal Trust, Pacific Forest Products, Concord Pacific, and the Toronto Stock Exchange.

In 2007, Brian was invited to be a fellow of the Canadian-based Institute of Corporate Directors. "That meant a lot to me," he says. "I worked hard to ensure that we did the right things at TELUS—and not just the things that seemed popular. My goal has always been to take the board of directors to a place where board meetings truly provide insight for the organization. I remember the days when a board meeting lasted two hours and involved little more than going over the financials. None of the other dimensions of a large and successful corporation were discussed. How far we've come since then.

"At the same time, it means a lot to me that there's a high degree of hierarchical transparency at TELUS. It used to be that there was relatively little communication between levels in this industry, but today people talk across hierarchical boundaries with little regard for what the levels between them actually are. That's unusual. They do it because it helps them get the job done, and I like to think that I helped to make that happen."

Brian's influence went far beyond the executive ranks. He also formal-ized a process through which key management personnel had the opportunity to provide their feedback about board members. During the sessions Brian scheduled with them, he would ask a battery of questions: What do you think of this particular committee? What do you think about the committee's chair—is the person effective? Do committee members address the topics you bring forward? Do they provide good guidance? What about the board as a whole—how can it serve the company better? What are your perspectives as a manager with regard to skill gaps on the board? This and other processes Brian instituted provided much more than simple assessment: they created a culture throughout the company that gave everyone a voice.

"Sometimes you just have to talk to people," Brian says. "The difference between commitment and indifference is understanding. If I'm seeking commitment from you and all I get is indifference, then it's incumbent on me to provide whatever is required to reach a point of understanding. I actually like contrarian people: they provide perspective. I'm on a number of corporate boards, and recently one of them was looking for an additional board member. One fellow expressed interest in being elected to the board, but the other members told me, 'We're not sure he's a good choice—he's very strong-willed and always expressing his own views.' Sounds good to me! Let's face it: if we all thought the same way, we'd be in nothing but trouble. I like people who come in and say, 'Have you thought about this?' 'Why not that way instead?' I've always believed that good leaders seek out different points of view, because those differences provide broader insight and understanding. Why *wouldn't* I want to hear different viewpoints?"

Brian has never been one to mince words, and especially not when it came to the governance of the organization. "The vice-chair of GTE," he recalls, "was a guy by the name of Kent Foster. He was a Texan. In the military he was an intelligence analyst, and he was a very bright engineer. One day, he was railing about something going on in Canada that was pertinent to the business, and I disagreed with his assessment of it. I can't recall what it was, but it was something I felt was not in the best interest of the company at the time. So I said, " 'You know, Kent, you can't make chicken soup out of chicken shit.' " His response was, 'That must be one of those quaint Canadian colloquialisms.' But I believe this: high-quality products and services require high-quality ingredients, and those ingredients include people, technology, and commitment."

A Man of the People

Bruce Canfield recalls a time when his father's disregard for hierarchy really came to the fore. During a labour strike at TELUS in 2005, Brian asked Bruce if he could be the second man on his repair truck. It was Bruce's first strike; he'd never experienced one before. He had been a cable splicer for ten years of his career, so he was assigned to perform that task as his strike assignment. Brian said to his son, "You're the boss. I'll do what you say. It's a role reversal, but that's okay."

"Needless to say, he was a magnet for the picketers," Bruce says. "Which could have been a problem. But it worked out great, because he kept them busy while I got the work done without incident. I'd get all packed up and ready to go, and he'd hop in the truck. But he kept them off my back. For him, it was the fifth work stoppage he had experienced. So while there were some exciting moments, for the most part it was pretty calm.

"There were also some very funny moments. At one point we went out to a job site, a new housing development that was going up, where I had to do some splicing. We went to the job site trailer, and the site supervisor let us in. Meanwhile, the picketers were pounding on the door and making a ruckus because they wanted us kicked off the site. But it turned out to be a non-union site, so we were allowed to stay. The supervisor said to my dad, 'So, what do you do when you're not on strike duty?' He responded, 'Well, actually, I'm the chairman.' The guy just about fell off his chair. The idea that the chairman of a company as large as TELUS would go out on strike

duty was just incredible to him. 'Well, fair enough—let's get you busy then!' the guy said."

Josh Blair tells a similar story from a different perspective. "When our board is together, we'll often invite senior vice-presidents and VPs two to three levels below the CEO to attend the annual strategy session," he explains. "It helps the vice-presidents understand what the board is doing, why they make the decisions they make. It also helps to guide them in their own jobs. The thing that struck me about those sessions is that I never saw Brian hanging out with the other directors; he visited only with the invited guests. He sat and talked with management, shared stories and advice, and listened to their perspective. It was good for them, because they got time with the chairman of the company, but it was also good for him, because he could gather insight from the people who work so hard to achieve the goals that were set by the board."

Brian believed that the most insightful leaders were those who talked with other employees at many levels, so he always made it a priority to tap into that knowledge base. Tracy White is a second-generation employee of the company, and she and her parents both remember being impressed by the extent to which Brian, during his time as CEO, mingled with the other employees. "We often saw him in the cafeteria shaking hands and joking like it was an average day for him. He was genuine and approachable."

The Governance Legacy

In 2005 and 2006, *Canadian Business* magazine's Top 25 Boards in Canada survey ranked the TELUS Board of Directors in the top ten. TELUS was the only telecommunications company to be included in the survey, which examines independence, accountability, total shareholder return, and disclosure. In January 2006, TELUS was recognized by IR *Magazine* as having the best corporate disclosure policy in Canada, based on a survey of 250 Canadian investment professionals. Thanks in large part to the efforts of Brian Canfield, TELUS continues to be a governance bellwether, setting ever-higher standards for corporate behaviour and challenging its peers to match them. The initiatives begun by Brian and undertaken by TELUS include:

- establishing a board diversity policy, which clearly stipulates the gender and racial makeup of the board;
- signing the Catalyst Accord, a commitment by major Canadian corporations to increase the board positions held by women to 25 per cent by 2017;
- adopting a term-limit policy that ensures the regular turnover of board members, as a way to bring fresh, innovative thinking to the board.

Not surprisingly, TELUS has been recognized for excellence in corporate reporting for 20 consecutive years by the Chartered Professional Accountants of Canada. The company's sustainable development and financial reporting disclosures received honourable mentions from the Dow Jones Sustainability World Index, and the 2005 TELUS Annual Report was recognized by the *Annual Report on Annual Reports* as the best annual report among public companies in the world on the basis of its layout and commitment to informational transparency. TELUS is one of only two Canadian companies to be ranked in the top ten globally for nine out of ten years by the same publication.

The list continues. TELUS received, from the Canadian Coalition for Good Governance, the 2013 Governance Gavel Award for the best disclosure of the approach to executive compensation, and the corporation received the award for the best sustainability, ethics, and environmental governance program at the first annual Canadian Society of Corporate Secretaries' Excellence in Governance Awards.

The initiatives attracting this acclaim started with Brian, but they haven't stopped with his departure—and they won't. "Brian has always been someone who brings things back to basic principles, back to that concept of being the 'chief commonsense

officer,' " says Darren Entwistle. "Those basic principles ensure that you don't get overly enamoured with a fad, whether it's a technology fad or a customer fad or a cultural fad. Brian taught us you must always be mindful that the basic business principles still hold true. For me, that meant differentiating ourselves from the competition, working our strategy back from the customer, understanding what's compelling to them, and always being mindful of those key components that drive our success."

As the new chair of the board, Dick Auchinleck will continue to lead with the transparency and innovation that have always guided TELUS in its business affairs.

A successful governance strategy depends in large part on the people who are in place to carry it to fruition, and Brian knew this better than most. "One of Brian's major legacies," says Micheline Bouchard, "was the recruitment of Darren Entwistle, and one of the most important responsibilities of a board is succession planning. Let's face it: it took some guts to hire a young man in his thirties to run a company as large and complex as TELUS. But Brian wasn't afraid of hiring a younger man. Brian put his trust in Darren, and Darren didn't let him down."

Mel Cooper appreciated Brian's commitment to the evolution of the company and the industry. "He had been through a lot," he recalls, "changing a company that was a monopoly into a strongly competitive entity, assembling a strongly cohesive company from a collection of regional entities, modernizing the infrastructure, and so on. He even tried to engage with the union, inviting the head union guy to come into the management team meetings so that he would know what was going on at the top of the house—he wanted the guy to be part of that. I've never seen that at any other company."

One of the decisions Brian, as chairman, made early in the game was to adopt computers at the board level. He felt it was important to embrace the technology and also to be in alignment with the company's commitment to be greener. At one point, he advised the board members that they would all be given a laptop, the first step in a commitment to having paperless board meetings. Some board members hadn't yet become comfortable with computers in their daily lives. But Brian persisted, making it clear that all meeting materials would be on the computer from then on—nothing would be printed. Mel Cooper arrived at one meeting with handouts he'd printed so he could read them on the plane during the flight to Vancouver. When Brian asked about it, Mel replied, "I printed them because I'm a Newfoundlander and even I'm capable of doing simple things." He then explained he wasn't comfortable reading confidential financial information on the plane on his computer, because it would be too easy for onlookers to see the numbers. "I don't think Brian bought it for a minute," says Cooper, "but he let it go. I'll tell you one thing, though: that was the last time I brought paper into one of his meetings."

Toward the Future

The Greek word *telesis* means "progress that is intelligently planned." Sociologists have adopted the term, identifying three forms of it: social

telesis, the informed direction of social activities to achieve a desired outcome; collective telesis, society's intent to achieve a particular end for the greater good; and individual telesis, which encompasses the deliberate actions taken by an individual to achieve personal growth and development.

Social telesis manifests itself at TELUS in numerous ways, including a corporate value statement that commits to spirited teamwork, and a commitment to governance that is second to none.

TELUS's engagement in the community, captured in the philosophy "We give where we live," speaks to the company's commitment to collective telesis. And TELUS's recognition of the contributions made by every employee says a great deal about the corporation's support for individual telesis.

Perhaps Brian Canfield's greatest gift to TELUS—among many—was his creation of a thoughtfully executed governance process that suffuses everything the company does, and informs the philosophy under which it operates. Governance, when done well, is telesis at its most effective.

Former senator Ross Fitzpatrick sums up Brian's legacy nicely: "If I were to teach a course in business ethics, I'd use Brian Canfield as a model. In every possible respect, he meets the test of ethical responsibility."

Brian presents a cheque for $1 million to Jeneece Place as part of TELUS's commitment to the community it serves.

CHAPTER 8

GIVING BACK

ZAJAC RANCH FOR Children is always a frenzy of activity as staff prepare for the summer season. Mel Zajac created the namesake facility to honour his two boys, who died in separate, tragic accidents. The ranch is situated on more than sixteen hectares of pristine forest on the shores of Stave Lake in Mission, British Columbia.

"At one time this place was a prison work camp," explains Zajac. "The prisoners would maintain trails, clean up the undergrowth in the forest, and do whatever needed doing as part of their sentences. The camps had barbed wire all around them, of course, but they also had dormitories and all kinds of buildings. At one point the government shut them down, so I bought one of them, this one, in 2003."

Zajac's original plan was to create a ranch that would be made available to underprivileged children through the foundation he had established in memory of his sons. At the time, Zajac lived near actor Paul Newman's brother, and when Zajac explained to him what he wanted to do with the camp, the brother suggested he contact Paul. Two days after sending Paul

FACING:
All in a day's work. Brian hauls gravel to a project at Zajac Ranch on the TELUS *Day of Giving (originally called the National Day of Service).*

an information package, Zajac heard from Newman's attorney, who wanted to arrange a meeting. Newman came to Vancouver, and he and Zajac toured the place. After listening to Mel Zajac's vision, Newman told Zajac he had to go one step farther, creating not only a recreational camp but also a medical facility. So he did. Zajac built a clinic and a small hospital, with a staff of thirty-six nurses and seven doctors. Soon, children with serious illnesses began to visit Zajac Ranch during the summer months for dialysis, chemotherapy, and other treatments. Once their treatments

were over, they were free to go outside and play. Today, during peak season, Zajac Ranch typically houses, treats, and entertains 450 to 500 kids in its nineteen buildings.

Brian Canfield's son Bruce remembers TELUS's initial involvement with Zajac Ranch. "When TELUS first started doing the TELUS Day of Giving in 2006 (originally called the National Day of Service), I volunteered out at the Zajac Ranch," he explains. "The ranch was still in start-up mode and wasn't running as well as it should, so as a volunteer I started looking for things that TELUS

could do to improve the facility. One of the things I really needed for my work up there were some heavy-duty landscaping tools, because the place is out in the wilderness, it's a big property, and the plants tend to run amok."

The TELUS Day of Giving provides a mechanism for the company to reach out across the entire country as a single, unified team, to make a positive and lasting difference in the communities where they live and work.

The effort is all volunteer, and thousands of employees and their families take part.

Bruce continues, "I remembered that my dad had this gas-powered hedge trimmer, which would be perfect. Zajac Ranch is huge, and you can't use electricity-powered tools unless you're prepared to walk around with a generator at your side all day. So I phoned him and asked if I could borrow his stuff for the weekend.

'Absolutely,' he responded. 'Of course you can borrow it, but what are you doing with it?' So I explained to him about the ranch and he said, 'Well, that sounds cool. Can I come with you?' And he did."

Every year since that first visit, Brian has brought a leadership team to work as a group at Zajac Ranch. Bruce now serves as the primary contact between TELUS and the ranch. He hosts the team, communicates with ranch staff, and organizes the employees who volunteer there on the annual TELUS Day of Giving.

Brian recalls his first visit to Zajac Ranch. "I was never so impressed as when I first went there and saw what they had done to make it possible for kids with disabilities to take part in the same physical activities that able-bodied kids could do," he recalls. "The pool, for example, is built like any swimming pool, except that at one end it has this artificial rock structure with what looks like

railway tracks leading into it. The kids who are in wheelchairs follow the train tracks through a crevice in the wall, and it takes them into a changing room. Then they come out in a different wheelchair that is specially designed so that it can go in the water without being damaged. From there, a track takes them down into the pool.

"They weren't able to put a retractable roof over the pool because it was expensive, and money is always a challenge for a facility like the ranch. So they did the next best thing. The roof is supported by a series of columns, and between every set of columns there's a garage door. In nice weather, the doors can be opened up to the outside. But the pool is just one aspect of the place. They also have a high-ropes course, canoeing, kayaking, archery, and a host of other activities."

Mel Zajac and Brian Canfield have become close friends over the years. "Brian's whole family comes to the ranch to work," says Zajac, "including his son, his son's wife and two grandchildren. Every time we have an event at the ranch, he has his whole family here.

"The first time I met Brian, he was at the ranch with a paintbrush in his hand, wearing coveralls. I went over and introduced myself and asked him, 'Are you one of the TELUS linemen?' He responded with a smile, 'No, I'm the chairman. And I brought my ex-CFO. He called me and asked if I wanted to go golfing; I suggested we go to the ranch instead.' "

"Yeah, that's sort of how it always is," Brian confirms. "I was up there working one day, shovelling muddy gravel, and these guys, part of an installation crew who were volunteering at the ranch on the TELUS Day of Giving, were up there working too. A lineman I had never met got out of his truck and came over, and said how nice it was to meet us in that

environment, that it meant a lot to him. I was working with a retired CFO, a guy who was still in shape enough to wheel gravel in a wheelbarrow. So it got away from designations and levels. We worked together that whole day."

"My dad sees Zajac Ranch as an important activity for himself and the company," Bruce Canfield muses. "He'll keep doing it as long as he can pick up a shovel. Besides, we're committed to the place in a big way, because it deserves our commitment. When TELUS first started working up there, we'd often have forty volunteers at the ranch at a time. As word of our commitment spread, others got interested. Then some of the telephone line crews got involved. The ranch is way up a gravel road, and when the line crews first visited, they came up with an idea. They said, 'The people in there really need Internet access.' They agreed to dedicate their time if TELUS would dedicate the fibre-optic facility and equipment. The company agreed, so these guys went in on their own time, with our equipment, and built the entire facility."

Brian's commitment to community has always gone well beyond his work with Mel Zajac and Zajac Ranch. In his role as an industry-sector leader, Brian helped create Vancouver's Science World, now the TELUS World of Science. He remains a patron to this day. He is a former honorary chairman of the Council of Governors of Leadership Vancouver, served as chair of the Business Council of British Columbia, served for eight years on the Royal Columbian Hospital Foundation's board of directors, and was a member of the cabinet of the United Way of the Lower Mainland. Brian was also a founder of the

Coquitlam Foundation, a non-profit organization that raises and allocates funds to community services, educational programs, and arts and culture initiatives. As president of the BC Summer Games from 1989 to 1991, he oversaw the planning and execution of its amateur sports competition in Coquitlam, bringing top athletes together from around the province. In 1992, Brian received the Commemorative Medal on the 125th anniversary of the Confederation of Canada for his decades of community work.

Brian participates in the TELUS Day of Giving (as the TELUS National

FACING:
Setting the example as he did, Brian didn't have to do much to inspire other TELUS team members to join him for a day of hard work at Zajac Ranch—or anywhere else, for that matter. This outside-plant team is running a high-speed network connection to the Ranch.

ABOVE:
Brian serves dinner to a group of TELUS retirees.

Day of Service is now known) every year, and he inspires others to do so as well. He maintains close relationships with the TELUS Community Ambassadors, a group of retirees and active team members who create backpacks full of school supplies for children in needy neighbourhoods, provide comfort kits filled with personal supplies for the homeless or those who have been evacuated because of natural disasters, and prepare bags filled with essential baby supplies for at-risk mothers, among many other activities. In 2010, TELUS was the first Canadian company to be named Most Outstanding Philanthropic Corporation in the world by the U.S.-based Association of Fundraising Professionals. In 2012, TELUS was selected as one of the winners of the inaugural Prime Minister's Volunteer Awards.

During his years with TELUS and beyond, Brian Canfield has shown by example how important and

rewarding community involvement can be. Perhaps former Coquitlam mayor Maxine Wilson captured it best in describing Brian's commitment to her city: "He demonstrated a dedication to the community through his hours of volunteering and his passion for making dreams a reality."

Mel Zajac echoes the mayor's comment. "TELUS has been really good to us," he says, "and I can see why—it's the leadership. Brian is humble, polite, charming, elegant, and he talks to everybody. I couldn't believe he was the chairman when he first started coming up here, because he was in there, elbow to elbow, up to his knees in mud, working with everybody else. He never shirks the work.

And it wasn't a one-time thing: he's been coming up for years. He asks for no favours, and he's always the first person there every morning. He jumps in, because he's just one of the guys waiting for his instructions for the day. In fact, he reminds me of one of my best friends, Bob Hope—he was very warm, and not the least bit arrogant. Brian has the same personality that he had. You just want to be his pal. We should have him running the country!"

ABOVE:
Mel Zajac, founder of Zajac Ranch.

FACING:
Darren Entwistle and Mel Zajac sharing a proud moment.

CHAPTER 9

THE FUTURE IS FRIENDLY

DESPITE MEL ZAJAC'S endorsement, Brian Canfield is too busy at the moment to consider taking on the leadership of Canada. Between the various corporate boards he sits on, his ongoing involvement with organizations like Zajac Ranch, the contraptions he invents in his machine shop with his plasma cutter, his home renovation projects, and playing golf in Palm Springs, spare time is at a premium.

Brian retired from TELUS—for the last time—on May 8, 2014. He left his position as chairman of the board the same way he had joined the company in 1956: energetic, engaged, and excited about what was yet to come.

"Five years ago," Brian says, "I wouldn't have guessed that TELUS would be in the business it's in today. It's amazing to think that we started out purely as a telephone company, yet today TELUS is in the process of becoming vertically integrated in so many ways. Just think about health care. It's a major part of what TELUS does, and the company will take that model right through to other verticals. The real trick will be to not get caught with stranded investment. Darren surrounded himself with a good

FACING:
When the TELUS Boot in Burnaby became the Brian Canfield Centre for Excellence in Telecommunications, this portrait of the man whose name the centre bears was commissioned.

team that helped him see the future and avoid the pitfalls that always come up."

One of Brian's major contributions to TELUS was his ability to prepare the leaders who succeeded him for the future that awaited. In the company's 2000 annual report, TELUS's new CEO, Darren Entwistle, stated, "TELUS is on track to lead the Canadian communications industry. We are evolving at a very fast pace because we understand that in this market, speed is of the essence and execution is everything." The numbers bore out his claims, as did the company's commitment to a path forward.

In his letter to shareholders in that report, Brian, as chairman, had this to say about the preceding year and the path ahead under Darren's leadership:

- We have a track record of achieving shareholder value and a new growth strategy focused on continued value creation in the future. In the last five

years, a $100 investment in TELUS has grown to $215, representing a total annual return, including reinvestment of dividends, of 17 per cent.
- Our strategy is clear and focused—our "100-day plan," announced in October 2000, has set the strategy that will lead us into the future. We will act in a manner that is consistent with this strategy.
- Our strategy is designed to define high-growth—we are focused on the high-growth areas of data, Internet Protocol (IP) and wireless, which will represent an increasing share of our revenue and value.
- We are the largest "pure play" Canadian telecom investment

opportunity—we will not be distracted and will only invest in business related to our core expertise.
- We have a talented management team—we have a renewed, high-powered management team, supported by a high-performance employee culture.
- Our strong telecom alliances enhance our core capabilities and build differentiation—we will continue to work with our world-leading partners, Verizon and Genuity, to provide our customers with the most advanced solutions.
- We have the financial strength to comfortably fund our growth ambitions—our strong balance sheet utilizes debt with investment grade

FACING:
Brian, his sons Brian and Bruce, and his grandson Drew on a hiking trip on the West Coast Trail in 2006.

ABOVE:
Brian's days in the executive suites may be over, but all indications are that he will be far busier retired than he ever was when he worked full time.

credit ratings to efficiently lever shareholder returns, and provides TELUS with the financial flexibility to wisely invest in new growth opportunities.

- Our performance targets reflect our growth profile—we have set clear and measurable targets to drive value. In 2001, we aim to deliver revenue growth of 17 to 19 per cent and EBITDA growth of 11 to 13 per cent.

Darren credits Brian's role in many of Darren's own successes as CEO, which took the company to new heights. Since 2000, TELUS shareholders enjoyed the highest total returns in the world among long-standing telephone companies, and the TELUS brand was rated number one in Canada for awareness and likeability by Léger Marketing. Perhaps the most important attribute Darren brought to the company was his skill with strategic diversification. Under his leadership, TELUS was the first telephone company in the world to build a nationwide, optical, all-IP backbone to meet transport needs,

including the delivery of entertainment and television to thousands of homes via the TELUS network. Darren's vision also led to the construction of the world's two most advanced data centres, in anticipation of a sea change that would lead the company deeper and deeper into the world of information technology. With the assistance of sixteen hundred physicians, nurses, and other medical professionals, the company launched TELUS Health, a move that has transformed health care by making TELUS the largest provider of electronic medical records in Canada. These developments, among many others, stand as a diversification indicator for other service providers throughout the world.

Darren recalls that Brian's help wasn't just at the professional level but at the personal level as well. "I wouldn't have the relationship with my family I have today if it weren't for Brian's guidance," says Darren. "You can't put a price on that. He was my supporter, a relief valve for the tough times that are part of the job. There were very few people I could talk to

about it, because they just didn't have the background, context, or understanding, but Brian did. I could talk to him, and he got it. Brian gave me the ability to purge the toxins from my system as a way to overcome the frustrations of the job—it was immensely valuable."

Over the years, TELUS has acquired a diverse range of highly specialized organizations that provide wireless services, Internet services, network security, professional services, videoconferencing, electronic medical records, consumer services, and much more—all part of the company's plan to offer a seamless service experience to its diverse business and consumer customer bases. At the same time, anticipating what lies ahead, the company has made enormous investments in infrastructure. As noted, TELUS was the first service provider in the world to build an all-IP backbone to transport its nationwide IP-based data services, and one of the first to build advanced MPLS (multiprotocol label switching) centres across the country as part of that effort. The two super centres the company added, in Kamloops in the west and Rimouski in the east, enjoy

From its humble beginnings, TELUS has become one of the most respected and admired corporations in the greater technology sphere.

the distinction of being the most advanced, energy-efficient data centres in the world.

"It's all about how you embrace the change," says Brian, "up to and including skipping a technology if it makes sense to do so. If you think about it, Gordon MacFarlane's time as CEO was all about that—getting us set up with the right technology and then setting us on a particular direction. My time as CEO was all about transitioning from a monopoly to operating in a healthy and fully competitive environment. Darren's time has been about geographic expansion and extensive diversification of the business. Ultimately, it's still all driven by scale and scope."

Industry analysts believe traditional websites may soon be replaced by downloadable apps that offer a personalized portal to access a company's products and services. Brian agrees. "Apps will be the future," he says. "Once there's a platform, people will write apps. And that's both good and bad, if you think about it, because apps are a form of over-the-top service, just like Netflix and iTunes. How do we compete with over-the-top in a world where everything we do is regulated, but the over-the-top providers are not? Regulation, while we can acknowledge the need for some of it, will hinder us. I used to have an expression: 'regulated competition.' That's an oxymoron if I ever heard one. That's the biggest bugaboo for this industry. Look, without too much work, you can get around all of the issues around stranded investment and financing challenges. But how do you get around regulatory practices that tie our hands behind our backs and then tell us to play catch?

"The original goal of regulation was to be a surrogate for competition—and that was a valid goal in a monopoly environment. The proper role of the CRTC was to protect consumers from a monopoly. But as competition matures, the need for strong regulation should fade. Today, we're in a highly competitive and mature telecommunications marketplace, yet we're often hobbled by outdated regulatory mandates that have been around since the days of monopoly.

Even so, we continue to do the right things for our customers to the best of our collective abilities. That's as true for our competitors as it is for us. For example, TELUS has made a commitment to bring service to the remote villages in the northern parts of the country. It isn't a government requirement; the company does it because it's the right thing to do for the people of Canada. It's an extraordinarily expensive proposition, but we don't see it as a choice. It's a social commitment, yet the regulators can't see fit to work with us on regulatory reform to make it easier to fulfill that commitment. That relationship has to change."

In his thinking on the industry, Brian is as forward-looking as ever. "I always come back to two things: technology and regulation. Technology is the mover and shaker, the change agent, the thing that never seems to stop. Regulation, on the other hand, always struggles to keep up. Technology always moves forward, which means that if you're going to stay competitive and relevant, you always have to *look* forward. The truth is,

everything is stochastic, because every moment is a variable. Everything's a moment of convergence.

"The thing that clicked for me was this. My entire career was dominated by the evolution from being the only game in town to operating effectively in a competitive environment. When I started with the company, it was a monopoly; when I left, it was fully competitive. During that period of time, the technology was the enabler of that change—it made everything we did possible. And the pace of its evolution was almost beyond comprehension.

"The thing is, this is not a cookie-cutter business. Things change all the time because there are so many variables. I *know* where I've been; what I *want* to know is where I'm going. But just as important, I want to know that if I know what's coming, I can act on that knowledge."

Brian's contributions as a leader in the complex and ever-changing telecommunications industry has been recognized on many levels, including numerous prestigious awards and accolades. BCIT awarded Brian an

*Former BC premier
Gordon Campbell,
Brian Canfield,
and the twenty-
seventh Lieutenant-
Governor of Brit-
ish Columbia, Iona
Campagnolo, at
the ceremony
inducting Brian
into the Order of
British Columbia
in 1998.*

honorary doctorate in 1997. When he was appointed to the Order of British Columbia in 1998, the accompanying citation noted, "As important as his business savvy has been to the economic development of British Columbia, Brian Canfield is a model corporate citizen." Brian was a recipient of a Queen's Golden Jubilee Medal in 2003, and in 2006 he was made a Member of the Order of Canada—the country's highest honour—for his lifetime of business achievement and service. "He is as admired for his

professional foresight and acumen as he is for spearheading community initiatives," the Order of Canada citation stated. In 2011, Brian received the Neotelis Canadian Telecom Career Service Award from the Telecommunications Hall of Fame. One aspect of Brian's character that everyone remarks on is that he never lost the connection with his roots. He remained a man of the people, in his work life and in his personal life as well. In a 2012 profile of Brian, *Business in Vancouver* magazine relayed a funny story told by former senator Ross Fitzpatrick:

> When [he] asked TELUS chairman Brian Canfield which resort he and his wife like to stay at when vacationing in California, Fitzpatrick was initially taken aback to learn that they stay in a fifth-wheel in an RV park.
>
> Mobile homes and RV parks seem such a plebeian pursuit for the chairman of a $10 billion company.
>
> "But when you stop and think of Brian and who he is, it really exemplifies what he is and where he came from, and the fact that he's never forgotten it," Fitzpatrick [says].

Jim Pattison, a self-made Canadian business legend in his own right, sees Brian as "a very self-effacing guy, and one of the finest representatives that the business community has in the whole of Canada. He's been there—meaning that he started from the ground up, started from the bottom of the pile, and learned some

Brian wearing his Order of British Columbia medal.

very important lessons on his way to the top. He's self-made all the way through and has never lost his humility, his sense of where he came from. I remember one time when I was flying home to Vancouver from a business trip, and I was in the back of the plane. And there was Brian as well, in economy. He's grounded—he walks the walk."

Bruce Canfield recalls that during his father's BC Tel days, the executives were all given company cars. The vehicles were also used as pool

cars for other employees and could be reserved for business purposes. His father's car was rarely available, however, because the trunk and backseat were always filled with tools. Even as TELUS CEO, Brian was busy doing home renovations and building projects in his spare time and on weekends. "Not much has changed over the years," says Bruce, "except that today his tools have got bigger."

This image of an ordinary guy who has no problem travelling in economy class, likes to get his hands dirty, and lives part of the year in a motor home is an interesting counterpoint to the visionary business leader who shaped TELUS to become a national company. There is absolutely no pretense to Brian Canfield. He is who he is: a man who understands how he got where he did, and who recognizes that he couldn't have done it alone. It takes a lot of people to sustain a successful organization. Industry is a team sport, and Brian has usually been the coach, rarely the quarterback.

TELUS, with its The Future Is Friendly brand and its Customers First strategy, has made a commitment to its customers, its shareholders, and its employees that it will do

everything in its power to harness the potential of the technologies it wields. Darren Entwistle's original mission statement, crafted as a vision for TELUS shortly after he joined the company, built on the work performed by Brian Canfield and those who came before him, and is carried on today: to unleash the power of the Internet to deliver the best solutions to Canadians at home, in the workplace, and on the move.

Unleash. What an appropriate word to describe this industry and its global impact, and what a perfect word to describe Brian Canfield's

contribution to it. Unleashed upon BC Tel in 1956 as a polisher of Bakelite telephones, he demonstrated over the course of fifty-eight years of service that hard work, commitment to a vision, empathy for those around you, and remembering where you started can lead to great things.

"Regulation, by design, won't keep up," says Brian, "but technology always has and always will get around all the challenges that are coming. And I for one can't wait to see what's over those next few hills."

Brian celebrates forty years with TELUS in the company of his family: son Brian Jr. and his wife, Kathy; daughter Nancy; wife Bev; son Bruce and his wife, Shelley; and grandchildren Drew and Hayley.

References

Written Sources

Angus, Ian. "Canadian Telecom Updates." Available at media.knet.ca/v/telemanagement/.

Benson, Don. *Wire Song: An Illustrated History of the Telephone in British Columbia, 1880–1930.* New Westminster, BC: Westminster Publishing, 1991.

Cuccia, Mark J. "Stentor Changes and History," July 7, 1999. Available at massis.lcs.mit.edu/archives/history/stentor.additional.history.

Equation project/Green ICT Initiative Trade Mission. "2 Key Sectors of Québec's ICT Industry," History of Québec Telecommunications, January 2014. Available at www.equationtic.com/wp-content/uploads/2014/01/Mission_Quebec-ICT-Profile-A4-V2.pdf.

Evans, Philip, and Thomas S. Wurster. *Blown to Bits: How the New Economics of Information Transforms Strategy.* Boston: Harvard Business School Press, 1999.

Ogle, E.B. *Long Distance Please: The Story of the TransCanada Telephone System.* Toronto: Collins, 1979.

Rey, R.F., ed. *Engineering and Operations in the Bell System.* Murray Hill, NJ: AT&T Bell, 1983.

SaskTel. "Stentor Alliance Restructures." September 18, 1998. Available at archive.is/FBGsS.

Sussman, Marsha. "Why HR Governance Matters." CEO Forum Group. Available at www.ceoforum.com.au/article-detail.cfm?cid=6287&t=/Marsha-Sussman-Mercer-Human-Resource-Consulting/Why-HR-Governance-Matters.

TELUS archives: Numerous uncategorized documents.

Interviews

The author conducted interviews with the following people on the dates shown:

Patti Armstrong, October 1, 2014

Josh Blair, April 25, 2014

Carol Borghesi, April 10, 2014

Micheline Bouchard, May 1, 2014

Brian Canfield (Sr.), April 11, 2014, and follow-up

Bruce Canfield, April 28, 2014

Deborah Cheslevy, September 10, 2014

Mel Cooper, May 1, 2014

Darren Entwistle, May 9, 2014

Ross Fitzpatrick, May 8, 2014

Professor Kyle Mayer, September 21, 2014

Jim Pattison, April 28, 2014

Lou Sekora, April 25, 2014

John Wheeler, April 29, 2014

Mel Zajac, April 28, 2014

Acknowledgements

ANYONE WHO KNOWS Brian Canfield knows that the man is larger than life and doesn't require much in the way of praise to demonstrate what a truly remarkable person he is. But many people contributed memories, stories, anecdotes, and moments that served to further enrich the tale told in these pages. My sincerest, most heartfelt thanks go out to each and every one of you.

First, thank you to the TELUS Board of Directors and Senior Leadership Team for undertaking this project and doing so much to make it real. Your recognition of Brian Canfield's accomplishments and contributions is noteworthy, but that's not unique in this project: TELUS goes out of its way as a corporation and as a member of the communities it serves to recognize both employees and customers for the special things they do to make the world a better place.

I offer a special thank-you to all the people who spent countless hours on the phone with me as I poked and prodded them for information. In alphabetical order I wish to thank Patti Armstrong, Josh Blair, Carol Borghesi, Micheline Bouchard, Bruce Canfield, Deborah Cheslevy, Mel

Cooper, Darren Entwistle, Ross Fitz-patrick, Professor Kyle Mayer, Jim Pattison, Lou Sekora, John Wheeler, and Mel Zajac. Thank you for your patience and your willingness to gen-erously share your time with me.

It bothers me that the author is typically the only person cited on a book's cover, and the person credited with doing all of the work required to create it. However, as the author, I can tell you that my efforts are part of a much larger effort, because without the skill and intellectual muscle of publishers, editors, graphic design-ers, and project managers, far fewer books would appear on shelves, and those that did would be far less read-able. My very special thanks, there-fore, go out to the Figure 1 Publishing team, including Lara Smith, Jessica Sullivan, Chris Labonté, Barbara Pulling, Judy Phillips, and Luci English. Thank you so much for your guidance, skill, creativity, and professionalism.

On the TELUS team, a special thanks to Dale Steeves, Nicola Was-son, Andrew Turner, Cindy Stewart, Sanja Todorovic, Georgia Doucette, Josh Blair, Karen Mackenrot, and Craig Volker for being the guiding force to keep us all on track. And a very special thank-you to Christine Larsen and Colin Tod, through whose tireless efforts the TELUS historical archives continue to yield magical insights about the remarkable history of the company and industry. Thank you for opening your archives and insights to me—I couldn't have done this without you.

Finally, thanks to Brian Canfield. I learned so much from you. We all did.

Photo Permissions

All photographs courtesy the TELUS Archives except:

page ix Gerry Kahrmann/*The Province*

page xiv Courtesy the Canfield family

page xviii Image used courtesy of New Westminster Museum and Archives, photo number IHP4912

page 3 Image courtesy of New Westminster Museum and Archives, photo number IHP92670218

page 4 Courtesy the Canfield family

page 5 Courtesy the Canfield family

page 7 Courtesy of The Computer Museum, Boston

page 8 Courtesy of IBM Archives

page 9 Photograph courtesy of the New Westminster Public Library. Photo by Don LeBlanc. NWPF photo number 629.

page 31 Courtesy the Canfield family

page 61 Courtesy the Canfield family

page 89 Courtesy Steven Shepard

Index

A

Alberta Government Telephones (AGT), 16,
 56, 61, 64
Allen, Paul, 45
American General Telephone & Electric
 Corporation (GTE), 18, 27, 90, 91, 97
Anglo-Canadian Telephone Company, 18, 90
AOL, 87
Apple Computer, 45
Armstrong, Patti, 6
ARPANET, 44, *44*
AT&T, 12–14
Auchinleck, Dick, 113
automatic direct dialing, 14–15
Automatic Electric Company, 27, 30, 38, 40
automatic switching, 27

B

Bakelite telephones, 22
Baldrige, Malcolm, 46
BC Summer Games and BC Seniors Games,
 104, 123

BC Tel (BC Telephone Company): and Brian Canfield (*See* Canfield, Brian at BC Tel); central
 office, 32–33; early days and structure, 14,
 17–18, 23; job fair, 9–10; management, 49;
 merger with TELUS Alberta, 65–67;
 Multiples Shops, 23; name change, 65;
 national toll system, 59; phone installation,
 21–22; restructuring, 50, 60, 65; the Shops,
 21–23; switching technology, 30; Technical
 Support, 51; vehicles, 10, *10*
BCT.TELUS, 66
BC Vocational School, 32
Bell Canada, 12, 18, 62; national expansion
 and competition, 63, 64, 66, 68–69
Bell Telephone Company, 15–16, 59–60
Blair, Josh, 36, 66–67, 68–69, 76, 101–2, *102*,
 111–12
Board of Railway Commissioners, 18, 54, 55
Bouchard, Micheline, 91–92, 99, *100*, 101,
 113–14
Brillant, Jules-André, 15
British Columbia, 2, 17–18

British Columbia Institute of Technology (BCIT), 32–33, 76, 133–34
Brotherhood of Electrical Workers Local 348, 67
Business in Vancouver, 134–35
business services, development, 45–46

C

Calder, Don, *65,* 66, 88
Campagnolo, Iona, *134*
Campbell, Gordon, *134*
Canadian Business magazine, 112
Canadian Coalition for Good Governance, 107–8
Canadian Pacific Railway, 2, 16, *55,* 59, 61
Canadian Pacific Telegraph, 59
Canadian Radio-Television Commission (CRTC), 18, 64, 132
Canadian Telephone & Supplies Ltd., 26
Canfield, Beverley (wife), 30, *31,* 32, *40,* 88
Canfield, Brian: adult education, 32–33, 37, 46, 76; on apps, 132; at BC Tel (*See* Canfield, Brian at BC Tel); on boards and in community initiatives, 108–10, 119–22, 123–25; at Canadian Telephone & Supplies Ltd., 26; career path, 72–73, *75;* and challenges, 79–81; and change and innovation, 76–79, 82–83, 85; character and skills, 6, 35, 37, 46, 71, 73, 134–36; commitment to work and customer, 73–74; computer programming, 36–37; contribution and awards, 133–35; and convergence in telecoms, 87–88; customer satisfaction, 35, 40, 49; and employees, 69, 71, 78, 81–82, 110–12, 121–22; and engineering economics, 35–36, 76; on governance, 109–10; infonet sessions, 71, 81–82; job fair in New West, 9–10; leadership and vision, 74–78, 79–83, 133–35; learning of management, 46; personal life (*See* Canfield, Brian, personal life); problem-solving qualities, 50–51; on regulation, 132–33, 137; retirement, xvii, *xvii, 75,* 127; and rewards-based meritocracy, 23, 73, 103; rise through BC Tel to Telus, xvi–xvii; and Stentor, 62–63; and success, xvi–xvii; and switching technology, 27, 30; on technology's role, 74, 133, 137; and Telecom Canada, 60–61; at TELUS (*See* Canfield, Brian at TELUS); and transparency, 82, 109; and Zajac Ranch, 119–22, 123
Canfield, Brian, personal life: children and family life, 32, 33, *40,* 41, *137;* interests and hobbies, 73; marriage, 30, *31;* as young student, 6–7; youth, *xiv,* 4–7, *6*
Canfield, Brian at BC Tel: as apprentice equipment installer, 11, 21–23; as area general manager, 50–51, 73; career path and rise through, xvi, xvii, *75;* in central office, 30–32; chairman and CEO, *54,* 65, 87; in DAISY project, 41, 44; early jobs and tasks, 26–27, 30; executive vice-president of Telephone Operations, 53; hiring of, 10–11; management and leadership development, 49–50; in Management Information Systems, 41; merger with TELUS Alberta, 66, 67; military client, 36, 37; network management, 36–38; as president and CEO/COO, 53, 60; in Sales, 46–49; as second-level manager, 38–39; supply chain work and management, 44, 46; as third-level manager, 44; in traffic engineering, 33, 35; TSPS and hotels, 38–40; as vice-president of Technical Support, 51; vision of future, 64

Canfield, Brian at TELUS: as CEO, 88, 90, 92,
    95, 132; as chairman, 87, 91, 95–97, 101,
    103–4, 105–7, 108, 113–14, 127; company
    cultures, 69, 95; contribution to, 127–28,
    133–34, 137; creation of TELUS, 66, 67, 69;
    and D. Entwistle, 95–97; governance, 92,
    99–101, 103–4, 105–6, 107–8, 109, 112–15;
    HR strategy, 103–4; and national expansion,
    90–91; and telecoms competition, 67–69;
    telesis, 115; and Telus's achievements and
    future, 128–30, 132–33; vision for, 68, 69,
    92, 96, 104, 113–14
Canfield, Brian (son), 32, *128*
Canfield, Bruce (son), *119, 128*; birth, 33; on
    father, 76, 81–82, 110–11, 135–36; and
    Zajac Ranch, 118–20, 122–23
Canfield, Drew (grandson), *119, 128*
Canfield, Effie (mother), 3, 4, *4*
Canfield, Francis (grandfather), 5, *5*
Canfield, Nancy (daughter), 41
Canfield, Orra (father), 3–4, *4, 5*
Cantel, 62
Chartered Professional Accountants of
    Canada, 112
Cisco, 87
City and Guilds of London Institute, 32–33
Colony of British Columbia, 2
Compagnie de Téléphone National, 15
competition in telecoms, 63, 64, 66–69, 74–75
competitive advantage, 45–46
computers, 8, 36–37, 44–45, *80*
Confederation broadcast, 59
Consent Decree of 1956, 12–14
CONUS Autovon, *34,* 36, 37
convergence in telecoms, 85, 86–88
Cooper, Mel, *93,* 93–94, 95, 108, 114
copper cable, *86,* 87

Coquitlam Foundation, 123
cord board, *26*
Corporation de Téléphone et de Pouvoir de
    Québec, 90
Customers First strategy, 135–36

D
DAISY project (Directory Assistance
    Information System), 41, 44
Deming, W. Edwards, 46
deregulation, 67–68
Diamond Jubilee broadcast, 59
direct dialing, 14–15, 19
directory assistance, 41, 44
Dominion Telegraph Company, 15
Douglas, James, 1
Dow Jones Sustainability World Index, 113
dual-class share structures, 107–8

E
Edison, Thomas, xv–xvi
Edmonton, Alta., 16
Edmonton District Telephone Company, 16
Edmonton Telephones Corporation (Ed Tel), 64
electronic switching, *39*
engineering economics, 35–36, 76
Entwistle, Darren, *22, 92, 124*; as candidate
    and interview, 94–95; as CEO, 21, 91, 92–93,
    95–97, 103, 113–14, 132; on role of Brian
    Canfield, 106, 113, 130–31; and Telus's
    future, 128–29; vision and role at Telus,
    130, 137
Ethernet, 45

F
Farrell, William, 17–18
Federation of Telephone Workers, 22

Fitzpatrick, Ross, 115, 135
forms for work, 77
Foster, Kent, 110

G
Gates, Bill, 45
Getting Rid of Dumb Rules (War on
    Waste), 77
gold rush, 1–2
Grand Metis Falls, 15
GTE, 18, 27, 90, 91, 97

H
Halse, George, 58
Haney Radio, 37
health care, and Telus, 130
high-tech industry. *See* technology in telecoms
hotels, and TSPS, 38–40

I
IBM Corporation, 8, 9, 10, 45
Institute of Corporate Directors, 109
Intel, 44–45
Internet, development, 44, 45
IP (Internet protocol), 86, 87; backbone,
    130, 131
IR Magazine, 112
IT, and telephone industry, 86

J
jacks and jack appearances, 23, *23, 25*

L
leadership of executives, xv–xvi, 83
Lester Pearson High School, 6, 8, *9*
long-distance calls, 19, 40, 56–60, 64, 85–86

M
MacFarlane, Gordon, *54, 80*; on Brian
    Canfield, 79–81; as CEO of BC Tel, 49,
    53, 78, 132
main distribution frame (MDF), *30*
management, developments in,
    45–46, 49
Manitoba Telephone System, 58, 59, 67
Mason Capital, 105–7
McKenney, H.W., 16
McKinsey & Company, 49–50
Microsoft, 45
microwave network completion, 19
microwave towers, *34*
MITS Altair, 45
Montreal Telegraph Company, 15
Monty, Jean, 62
Moody, Richard Clement, 1–2
multiples, 23

N
National Day of Service. *See* TELUS Day
    of Giving
Neotelis Canadian Telecom Career Service
    Award, 134
Newman, Paul, 117–18
New Westminster, *xviii,* 1–3; Canfield family
    in, 3–7
New Westminster and Burrard Inlet
    Telephone Company, 17
Northern Electric (Nortel Networks), 12
North-West Telephone Company, 18

O
Oliver, Frank, 16, 18
Order of British Columbia, 78, 134, *135*
Order of Canada, 134

P

Pattison, Jim, 135
PBX (Private Branch Exchange), 47–49, *48*
Pertch, Larry, 5
Peters, Tom, 45–46
Petty, George, 65, 88
Porter, Michael, 45
provinces, 56–59, 61, 63

Q

Quebec province, 90
Québec-Téléphone/QuébecTel, 15, 90–91, 97
Queen's Golden Jubilee Medal, 134

R

railroad industry, 16, 54–55, 58
Railway Act (1903), 18
RAMAC (Random Access Method of Accounting and Control), *8*
regulation, 12, 18–19, 54–56, 132–33
resellers, 64
Rogers, Ted, 61, 62

S

Sekora, Lou, 104
services convergence, 87
Stentor Alliance/Stentor Canadian Network Management, *61*, 62–64, 67
step-by-step office/switch, *20, 27*, 30
Stinson, Bill, 61
Strowger, Almon, 27, *27*
switching, *20, 27*, 30, 32, *39*

T

TAT-1 transatlantic telephone cable, 8
Taylor, Alex, 16, 18
technology in telecoms: beginnings and expansion, 7–9, 18–19; computers and IT, 36–44; convergence in, 86–87; and employees, 72; importance and role, 21, 74, 133
Telecom Canada (formerly TCTS), 60–62, *61*
telecommunications industry: change in, 85; competition, 66–69; complexity, 51; convergence in, 85, 86–88; deregulation, 67–68; early 1980s, 46–47; employees and work culture, 68–69, 71–72; governance, 99; network development, 46–47; regulation, 54–56, 132–33; resellers in, 64; technology (*See* technology in telecoms). *See also* telephone industry
Telecommunications Workers Union, 67
Telephone Association of Canada (TAC), 58, 59
telephone cable, early days, 8, *24*
telephone industry: change in, 85–86; diversity in, 55–56; early days to 1956, 12–15, 27; governments as operators, 56–59; history in Canada, 15–16; national system, 56–60; regulation, 12, 18–19; service development, 38
telesis, 114–15
TELUS: achievements and future of, 105–6, 128–30, 131–33, 136–37; annual report, 113; board of directors, 99–101, 103–4, 105, 106–7, 109, 112, 114; the Boot, 81–82; as brand, 130; and Brian Canfield (*See* Canfield, Brian at TELUS); CEOS, 91–97; Clearnet acquisition, 88, 91, 97; community initiatives, 115; company cultures, 69, 95, 96; and competition, 67–69; corporate disclosure, 112; data centres, 88, *89,* 131–32; early history, 64–65; employees and HR, 102–4; engineering economics, 76; foreign ownership, 104–5; governance, 100–104, 107–8, 112–13, 115; long-term view, 105–6; merger

of BC Tel and TELUS Alberta, 65–67; name
and headquarters, 66; national expansion,
90–91, 92, 96–97; and national service,
67–69; risk management, 103; shares and
shareholders, 99–100, 104-7, 130; strike of
2005, 110–11; and technological change, 92,
94; telesis, 115
TELUS Alberta/TELUS AGT, 64, 65–67
TELUS Community Ambassadors, 124
TELUS Day of Giving, 118, 119, 120, 123–24
TELUS Health, 130
TELUS Québec, 90
TELUS World of Science, 123
The Future Is Friendly brand, 135–36
Theodore Gary and Company, 18
toll system, 59–60
Total Quality Management, 46
traffic engineering, 35–36
Trans-Canada Telephone System (TCTS), 60, *60*
TSPS (Traffic Service Position System), *38,*
38–40
TX-0 (Transistorized Experimental computer
zero), *7, 7*–8

U
unions, 22–23, 67
United States, 12

V
Verizon, 91
Vernon and Nelson Telephone Company, *17*
Victoria and Esquimalt Telephone Company, 17

W
War on Waste (Getting Rid of Dumb Rules), 77
Waterman, Robert, 45–46

Wheeler, John, 63
White, Tracy, 112
Wilson, Maxine, 125

X
Xerox, 45

Z
Zajac, Mel, 117–18, 121, 123, *124,* 125, *125*
Zajac Ranch for Children, *116,* 117–23,
118, 119, 120, 122